Bond

The Parents' Guide to the 11+

Michellejoy Hughes

Nelson Thornes

Published in 2006 by:
Nelson Thornes Ltd
Delta Place
27 Bath Road
CHELTENHAM
GL53 7TH
United Kingdom

11 12 / 10 9 8 7 6 5 4 3 2 1

A catalogue record for this book is available from the British Library

ISBN 978 1 4085 1582 2

Cover photograph: Hammock by Doug Menuez/Photdisc 38A (NT)
Page make-up by Wearset Ltd, Boldon, Tyne and Wear

Printed in Croatia by Zrinski

The Parents' Guide to the 11+

Contents

Notes on the author

Michellejoy Hughes is a qualified and experienced teacher. She studied for her BA and PGCE in English at Liverpool and then her MA in English at Lancaster. She has spent many years working as a teacher in Liverpool, preparing pupils for SATs, GCSEs and A-level exams and she has worked as an examiner in English.

Michellejoy has written numerous articles and here she combines her experience and knowledge in an easy to read step-by-step manual for parents whose children will be sitting the 11+ examination.

Michellejoy now teaches the 11+ privately and tutors over 30 pupils a week. Her pupils represent private, selective and state schools and a whole variety of backgrounds. Some parents have been through the system before whilst others have no prior knowledge of the 11+ and all parents want to know whether their child actually stands a realistic chance of passing the 11+.

In order to prepare for the 11+, Michellejoy has used the Bond series to devise a range of initial Placement Tests which are provided here as a detachable section to test your child. She has also created numerous teaching and motivational aids which she shares in this book.

Having real solutions that are used in practice every week to great success, is a key element of this book. Michellejoy shares solutions to common problems and using this manual will ensure your child receives the best preparation in order to pass the 11+.

◄ *My child was doing well enough at school but we knew he wouldn't pass the 11+ without some help and guidance. We came to Michellejoy and our son followed the easy step-by-step methods and he really enjoyed the learning experience. He was well prepared for the 11+ exam and we were thrilled when we received the results and he passed. He is now settled happily into the grammar school and we would whole heartedly recommend the teaching methods used.* ►

Introduction
The Bond 11+ Action Plan

Step 1
Understand the 11+

Find out about the 11+

Understand the subjects involved

Recognise the skills tested for

Ascertain when and where the 11+ takes place

Step 2
Assess your child

Find out if your child should sit the 11+

Determine your child's ability

Kick-start your preparations with the Bond Placement Tests

Test and mark your child

Step 3
Prepare for the exam

Follow the unique step-by-step strategy plans

Discover how to motivate your child

Learn the secrets of controlling stress

Work through the exam day itself

Step 4
Manage the post-exam process

Understand what happens next

Find out about the results and appeals process

Prepare for secondary school

Manage stress

What is the 11+?

How do I decide if my child should take the 11+?

How do I prepare for the 11+ exam?

What happens after the exam?

You've heard whispers about the 11+ and some parents already have their children with private tutors and the practise books available overwhelm you. What is it all about and what can you do to best prepare your child?

This book will take you step-by-step through the whole 11+ examination process. The detachable Placement Tests and easy marking scheme provided in this manual will help you to assess your child and to build a picture of their ability.

The exam strategy plans will guide you through the exam preparation whether you have 12 months, 6 months or 3 months, with advice if you have more or less time before your child sits the 11+ exam. The process includes tips to manage stress and to maintain motivation and helps to make this important time exciting and enjoyable for everyone.

This manual takes into account regional differences and the types of 11+ tests your child will take. Whether it is an LEA or selective grammar/private school 11+ exam, you can find out what is expected of your child and of you. The book also guides you through the post-examination process and will help to prepare your child for secondary school.

The Parents' Guide to the 11+ provides the answers to your questions and will take the mystery and confusion out of the 11+. Following this manual will help to provide the best chance your child has at passing the 11+ exam and beyond.

STEP 1

Understand The 11+

> ❝ I've overheard some of the parents talking about the 11+ and I know it's a test, but other than that, I'm not really sure what it's all about. The whole secondary school process seems confusing and I don't know who to talk to about it. I'm not even sure what questions I need to ask! ❞

> ❝ I've been on the Internet but I spent all night and still didn't find what I was looking for. You go into a bookshop and there are loads of workbooks for the children but nothing for parents. ❞

1

What is the 11+?

The 11+ is a selective entry examination for secondary school that children sit during their school Year 6. For some Local Education Authorities (LEAs), the 11+ is available for all Year 6 children and the exam is taken during the school day in their primary school. In other parts of the country, the 11+ is organised by the selective and private schools and the exam is taken after school or on a weekend and takes place at the senior school. The 11+ is a means of testing children from an academic perspective and has no bearing on their SATs or GCSEs. Until the early 1970s, all children took the 11+. It is no longer a compulsory test but it continues to be used by the grammar and selective schools.

The 11+ exam differs throughout the country in terms of the subjects taken and also the examining board used. There are four subjects that can be tested in the 11+ exam. The subjects are verbal reasoning, non-verbal reasoning, English and maths. Although the maths and English tests tend to follow the National Curriculum, the verbal and non-verbal reasoning tests are not school-based subjects. Further information about the subjects tested can be found later in this section.

All of these tests can be either standard format (SF), or multiple-choice (MC). The standard format is an exam paper that asks questions and has a space beneath for the response. In a multiple-choice exam, there is a separate answer sheet consisting of boxes of potential answers for every question. Each child makes a mark next to the box they think is correct. With the standard format, a child cannot guess so easily, but the answers are all on the same sheet. In multiple-choice, a child can guess but there is the need to accurately mark off answers on the answer sheet.

When and Where is the Test?

HINT

It is vital that you confirm with your choice of school when the 11+ is and what subjects are tested as LEAs do change 11+ exam board and this can mean a different time of year, different subjects and different formats of examination.

Not all subjects are covered in every regional area so here is a guide to the LEAs and the subjects they test at 11+, with the time of year that they offer the 11+ exam. Some LEAs are listed more than once, which corresponds to different grammar schools. For specific schools' information and for your LEA's contact details, see Appendix D found at www.bond11plus.co.uk in the Free Resources section. The following overview of LEAs and 11+ details was correct at time of writing but is always subject to change.

LEA	ENGLISH SF	ENGLISH MC	MATHS SF	MATHS MC	VR SF	VR MC	NVR SF	NVR MC	Exam month
Barnet		✓		✓	✓			✓	Nov
Barnet	✓	✓							Jan
Bexley				✓	✓				Sep
Birmingham		✓		✓		✓		✓	Nov
Birmingham	✓		✓		✓				Nov
Birmingham			✓				✓		Oct
Bournemouth		✓		✓	✓				Nov
Bournemouth		✓		✓	✓			✓	Nov
Bromley	✓		✓		✓		✓		Nov
Buckinghamshire						✓			Oct
Calderdale	✓			✓	✓				Dec
Calderdale				✓		✓			Dec
Cumbria				✓	✓			✓	Jan
Devon		✓		✓	✓				Oct/Nov
Essex	✓		✓			✓			Nov
Gloucestershire						✓			Nov
Hertfordshire			✓		✓				Nov/Dec
Kent	✓		✓		✓				Sep
Kent						✓			Sep
Kent		✓		✓		✓		✓	Sep
Kent							✓		Sep
Kent		✓		✓		✓		✓	Sep
Kent				✓		✓		✓	Sep
Kent				✓		✓		✓	Sep
Kent		✓		✓		✓		✓	Sep
Kent	✓		✓		✓				Sep
Kingston upon Thames						✓		✓	Dec
Kirklees				✓		✓		✓	Dec

LEA	ENGLISH SF	ENGLISH MC	MATHS SF	MATHS MC	VR SF	VR MC	NVR SF	NVR MC	Exam month
Lincolnshire					✓			✓	Sep
Liverpool	✓		✓					✓	Oct
Medway	✓			✓	✓				Oct
North Yorkshire	✓		✓		✓		✓		Oct
North Yorkshire					✓			✓	Oct
North Yorkshire						✓		✓	Sep
Plymouth	✓			✓	✓				Jan
Poole						✓		✓	Nov
Poole		✓		✓	✓				Nov
Reading					✓		✓		Nov
Reading	✓		✓		✓	✓	✓	✓	Nov
Redbridge						✓		✓	Dec/Jan
Slough							✓	✓	Nov
Slough			✓		✓			✓	Nov
Southend-on-Sea	✓		✓		✓				Nov
Stoke-on-Trent					✓		✓		Sep
Sutton			✓		✓				Nov
Sutton	✓			✓	✓				Nov
Sutton	✓		✓		✓				Sep
Sutton	✓			✓	✓				Jan
Telford and Wrekin					✓	✓		✓	Jan
Telford and Wrekin						✓			Dec
Torbay	✓		✓		✓				Nov
Trafford		✓	✓			✓			Sep
Trafford	✓			✓		✓		✓	Sep
Trafford				✓		✓		✓	Sep/Oct
Trafford	✓			✓				✓	Oct
Trafford	✓			✓	✓				Sep
Walsall						✓		✓	Dec
Warwickshire	✓		✓		✓		✓		Oct
Wiltshire			✓		✓	✓			Nov
Wirral						✓			Nov/Dec
Wolverhampton			✓		✓	✓		✓	Nov

Private Schools

The private schools will differ, as they will use either their own exam or the 'Common Entrance Exam'. This is a written test of maths, English and science. If a private school is using the Common Entrance Exam, the examination date is in January but do contact the schools in plenty of time to check whether they use this or set their own examination and to confirm time of year. This information is usually in their current school prospectus. It is usually possible to get past papers from the school to use as revision. See Appendix D (found at www.bond11plus.co.uk) for the contact details of private schools.

Which Subjects Does the Exam Cover?

Verbal Reasoning

Verbal reasoning tests are popular as they are a good indication of potential academic ability. They test whether a child can problem solve, whilst working quickly and accurately, and how effectively they can process verbal information. But what does this really mean? Verbal reasoning tests can be broken into four sections: Sorting Words, Selecting Words, Anagrams and Coded Sequences.

- Identify groups of words
- Sort words into categories
- Pair up words
- Find words that do not belong
- Find words that are most similar
- Find an opposite word
- Find words that have letters in common

- Make compound words
- Choose pairs of opposites
- Finish one word and begin the next
- Find a prefix for a set of words
- Make new words by removing letters
- Make new words by adding letters
- Transfer letters to make new words

Sorting Words | **Selecting Words**

Anagrams | **Coded Sequences**

- Rearrange letters to make a word
- Rearrange a sentence to make sense of it
- Use a rule to create new words
- Complete crosswords
- Put words in alphabetical order
- Find a word hidden in a sentence
- Find a small word in a larger word

- Work out letter and number sequences
- Code and decode words using letters
- Code and decode words using numbers
- Code and decode words using symbols
- Make deductions from given information
- Apply number logic

Let's have a look in more detail at each section and understand how you can help your child succeed at Verbal Reasoning.

Sorting Words

This section is all about word recognition and definition. Can your child identify words that are similar or different? Out of a given group of words can your child work out which is the odd one out? Some questions require a child to organise words into categories or to find a common link between words. Below are some examples of sorting words questions.

(1) In these questions, your child is asked to select the best-fit answer.

> **Q** Big is to small as tall is to (narrow, short, high).
> Jumper is to wool as shirt is to (cotton, white, smooth).
> Cat is to kitten as horse is to (calf, foal, animal).
> *Answers: short, cotton, foal.*

HINT

Common problems stem from a lack of word knowledge. Reading, word games and dictionary games will help your child to answer these types of questions.

The skill required here is for your child to have an understanding of the **relationship** between words, to be able to put words into pairs and to recognise opposites, similarities or how words are connected in some way.

The strategy needed is for your child to keep asking, 'What is the link between the first pair?' When they can find the answer, 'Big is opposite to small', they need to keep the same pattern in the second set of words, 'Tall is opposite to short'.

> **TRY THIS!**
>
> Play word games with your child where you suggest a word and tell them to find a word that is opposite and then similar to it, or a game where you suggest a pair of words and your child tries to find the common link. This can really help with the second example here where a child might know that jumper and wool are not opposite or similar but if they can find another link, i.e. Jumpers can be made out of wool, the following pairing is made easier.

(2) In these questions, the aim is to select two words (one from each group) that are most similar.

> **Q** (liquid, soft, fixed)   (rough, fluid, melt)
> (sing, melody, music)   (laugh, instrument, tune)
> (dear, customer, buy)   (expensive, gift, present)
> *Answers: liquid/fluid, melody/tune, dear/expensive.*

The skill required here is knowledge of vocabulary and synonyms; to know the definition of words and which ones are most similar in meaning. The strategy here is to pair the first word of the first bracket with the words in the second bracket and then the second word of the first bracket with words in the second bracket, etc.

For example:

Liquid is rough, liquid is fluid, liquid is melt.
Soft is rough, soft is fluid, soft is melt.
Fixed is rough, fixed is fluid, fixed is melt.

Which makes most sense? At least some of these statements can be rejected.

For example:

liquid is rough, soft is rough, fixed is rough
None of these make sense and so rough cannot be the link word.

Liquid is melt, soft is melt, fixed is melt
None of these are right so melt cannot be the link word, which leaves us with fluid. Now which of the first bracket words is most like fluid?

Liquid is fluid, soft is fluid, fixed is fluid
We know it cannot be fixed or soft so we have our answer.
Liquid is fluid.

▐▶ TRY THIS!

Good techniques for your child:
1 Always use a pencil so that changes can be made.
2 Read each question thoroughly so that you do not misunderstand what to do. If there is an example given, make sure you understand it.
3 Work logically from left to right to create a systematic order.
4 Until you are practising for speed, always check your answers and as you build up speed, still try to use a checking process.

③ In these questions, your child is asked to select the two odd words out.

> Q (blue, sky, white, clouds, green)
> (toffee, coffee, sweets, milk, tea)
> (football, kit, player, cricket, rounders)
> *Answers: sky/clouds, toffee/sweets, kit/player.*

The skills required here are to find the common link between words and the ability to recognise the most appropriate link between groups of words. The strategy can be difficult for the more creative child, as it can be easy to find links. For example, in the first question a child might choose 'green' and 'clouds' as the odd words out because the sky is blue and white, or they might select 'green' and 'white' because the sky is blue and has clouds. It is therefore important for the child to consider which link provides a definite group, e.g. blue, white and green are all colours therefore sky and clouds are the odd ones out. It isn't just about finding any linking word; it is about finding the **strongest** link between the group.

Selecting Words

This section is about recognising how a word can be constructed. Does your child understand how to make compound words or add a prefix and suffix to a root word? Can your child add two words together to make a compound word or make new words by removing or adding a letter?

HINT

Definitions

Root word	A word without a prefix or suffix.	state, form, happy
Prefix	Letters added to the beginning of a word.	<u>under</u>state, <u>re</u>form, <u>un</u>happy
Suffix	Letters added to the end of a word.	state<u>ment</u>, form<u>ation</u>, happi<u>ness</u>
Compound word	Two words added together to make a new word.	tea + spoon = teaspoon ring + let = ringlet

Below are some examples of selecting words questions.

1 Find one word from each group that when added together, make a compound word.

> (over, out, above) (side, under, way)
> (fair, dark, black) (apple, berry, tree)
> (down, up, out) (let, give, over)
> *Answers: outside, blackberry, outlet*

The skill required here is knowledge of vocabulary and how words can be created. Understanding root, prefix and suffix elements of a word and how compound words can be created is important for these types of questions.

The strategy here is to take each word from the first bracket and to pair it with each word of the second bracket to create a logical system working from left to right. For example:

overside, overunder, overway
outside, outunder, outway
aboveside, aboveunder, aboveway

A child will usually find the correct answer as they go through this process but if they do become stuck, at least they can reject the worst sounding pairs and then make a logical guess at the compound word.

2 Move one letter from the first word and add it to the second word to make two new words.

> plume   rat
> feather   had
> stick   no
> *Answers: plum/rate, father/head, sick/not.*

The skill required here is word knowledge and spellings. The strategy is to use a logical system, so starting at the left, remove each letter one at a time from the first word to see if the remaining word makes sense. If it does, try adding the removed letter to the second word to see if a new word can be created. For example:

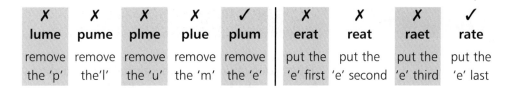

✗	✗	✗	✗	✓	✗	✗	✗	✓
lume	pume	plme	plue	plum	erat	reat	raet	rate
remove the 'p'	remove the 'l'	remove the 'u'	remove the 'm'	remove the 'e'	put the 'e' first	put the 'e' second	put the 'e' third	put the 'e' last

③ Find a word that will prefix all of the words in the brackets.

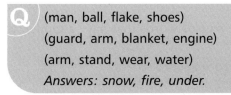

> **Q** (man, ball, flake, shoes)
> (guard, arm, blanket, engine)
> (arm, stand, wear, water)
> *Answers: snow, fire, under.*

The skills required here are vocabulary knowledge and creativity. The strategy is to again use a logical left to right system, but this time creating compound words. The difference is that there is only one word in the answer and this can cause much difficulty in trying to find the link word.

One technique is to take each word in the brackets and create as many words as possible that include this word. For example:

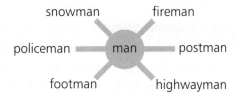

Systematically apply each word to the others in the brackets to look for a match and reject those that don't work as you go.

It is clear from this process that snow is the common word and so it must be the link we are after.

Finding a starting place is often difficult for a child so a technique might be to learn a list of compoundable words. Here are some common headings and words that might be included under each heading:

Elements	Positions	Colours	Body parts
snow	under	green	eye
rain	over	white	leg
wind	back	black	arm
sun	front	blue	foot
fire	in	red	hand
earth	out	gold	lip
ice	side	brown	head
water	left		mouth
hot	right		toe
cold	down		finger

Does your child know the alphabet? Can they recognise words that have been switched around or are hidden in a sentence? Can they use a logical rule and apply it to other words? Below are some examples of anagram questions.

(1) Find the pair of words that have a hidden four-letter word between them.

> **Q**
> I have to visit my aunty.
> The dog ate the tinned food.
> He drove the children to school.
> *Answers: have – to (veto), dog – ate (gate), children – to (rent).*

The skills required here are knowledge of vocabulary and spellings. The strategy here is to start at the left and, working systematically, look at all groups of four-lettered words that are placed at the end of each word and the beginning of the next until a word is revealed.

> **IIII➤ TRY THIS!**
>
> It can be helpful for your child to use their fingers to cover up the other letters and to silently say, as well as look, at the potential words available.

(2) Find the missing three-letter word that needs to be added to the other letters to create a correctly spelt word.

> **Q**
> The boy put on his SS.
> She went to the shop and bought chocolate and STS.
> They were fishing for TR.
> *Answers: HOE (shoes), WEE (sweets), OUT (trout).*

The skills required here are knowledge of extended vocabulary, an ability to spell and to recognise the context of a word in relation to others. The strategy here is for your child to read the sentence carefully and to then decide what answers will fit in the blank space. Each word selected should then be checked against the letters available to see if there is a three-letter word that will fit. This is often a difficult question for children to attempt.

One successful technique is to think of all potential words that are linked to the rest of the question. For example, 'The boy put on his SS'.

Now check if each word fits with the letters given and see which letters are left over. Do you have a three-letter word that makes sense?

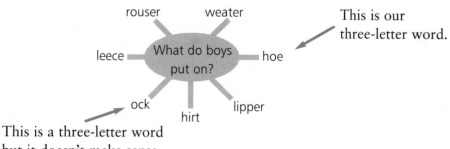

rouser   weater

This is our
three-letter word.

leece — What do boys put on? — hoe

ock

hirt   lipper

This is a three-letter word
but it doesn't make sense.

(3) The words in the second group should be put together in the same way as the words in the first group. Can you find the words missing in the second group?

> **Q** (master – male – learn)   (rest – ? – apple)
> (bugle – ugly – fairly)   (girl – ? – upon)
> (play – sway – swim)   (look – ? – bore)
> *Answers: reap, iron, book.*

The skill required here is an ability to follow patterns and to recognise the order of letters within a word. The strategy for answering this type of question is to try numbering each letter to find which number sequence is used and then copy it for the second group of words.

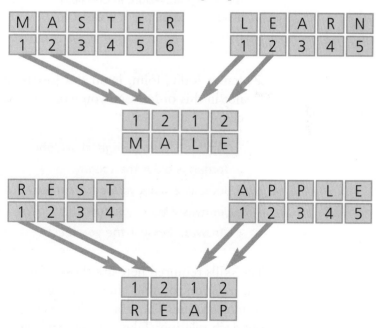

✓ HINT

Sometimes the same letter can be found in both words (such as the A in MASTER and LEARN), so remind your child to be careful. Only one sequence will correctly spell a missing word.

M	A	S	T	E	R
1	2	3	4	5	6

L	E	A	R	N
1	2	3	4	5

1	2	1	2
M	A	L	E

R	E	S	T
1	2	3	4

A	P	P	L	E
1	2	3	4	5

1	2	1	2
R	E	A	P

Another technique that can be used is to try underlining which letter is used and in which order and repeat this letter by letter for the second word.

M = 1st letter 1st word   **R** = 1st letter 1st word

A = 2nd letter 1st word   **E** = 2nd letter 1st word

L = 1st letter 2nd word   **A** = 1st letter 2nd word

E = 2nd letter 2nd word   **P** = 2nd letter 2nd word

Codes and Sequences

This section develops the placement and order of words and sentences. Can your child understand letters exchanged for numbers? Can they link letters with replaced symbols? Can they understand critical information from a series of sentences? Typical code and sequence questions are given below.

(1) If A = 1, B = 2, C = 4, D = 8 and E = 12 write the answer as a letter.

> **Q**
> C + D =
> C × B =
> E − D =
> *Answers: E, D, C*

The skills required for this question are an ability to interchange letters and numbers and to understand how substitution works. The strategy for this question is to rewrite the equation exchanging numbers for the letters, work out the sum and then convert the numbers back to letters.

> **▶ TRY THIS!**
>
> It is easy for your child to get flustered and confused with this type of question. It requires logical thinking and the ability to carry out the whole procedure in one fluid action. For example, it is easier to think:
>
> C is 4 and D is 8 and 4 + 8 = 12, which is E, than thinking C + D means C = 4 and D = 8 and so C + D = 4 + 8 which = 12 and 12 is the letter E.

(2) Jenny, Jodie, John, Jamil and Jordan are 10, 9, 8, 7 and 6 years old but not in this order. Can you work out who is the youngest from these clues?

> **Q**
> Jamil is 1 year younger than John.
> Jordan is older than Jenny.
> Jodie is 2 years younger than John.
> Jenny is 2 years younger than Jodie.
> *Answer: Jenny is the youngest.*

The skills required here are those of logic, being able to recognise facts that bear relation to other clues and the ability to deduct maximum information from each clue. The strategy here is to create a logical system for working out each relation. Take each sentence and, in turn, work out all the information that can be gained from it.

Jamil is 1 year younger than John so:
- Jamil cannot be 10.
- John cannot be 6.
- The youngest cannot be John.

Jordan is older than Jenny so:
- Jordan cannot be 6.
- Jenny cannot be 10.
- The youngest cannot be Jordan.

Jodie is 2 years younger than John so:
- Jodie cannot be 9 or 10.
- John cannot be 6 or 7.
- Jamil cannot be 6.
- Jamil cannot be the youngest.

Jenny is 2 years younger than Jodie so:
- Jodie cannot be 6 or 7.
- Jenny cannot be 9 or 10.
- Jodie cannot be the youngest.

We now know that Jenny must be the youngest as she is the only one left.

In a timed exam, children often struggle with this type of question, so the important thing to remember is to draw a quick grid straight away and mark the boxes as you read each statement, bearing in mind the question the whole time. For example, in the grid below, after each statement such as 'Jamil is older than John' you could put an 'x' in the 'Age 6' row under Jamil and in the 'Age 10' row under John.

HINT

Most newsagents sell logic puzzle books based on various grids and tables and these are great practice not only for these types of questions, but also for developing logical and systematic thinking. They are great as time fillers for car journeys and waiting rooms!

	Jamil	John	Jordan	Jenny	Jodie
Age 10	x			x	x
Age 9				x	x
Age 8					
Age 7		x			x
Age 6	x	x	x		x

It is easy to consider other pieces of information. For example in the above question, you could work out how old everyone is, but the question only requires you to know who the youngest is. You are looking for the name who doesn't have an 'x' in the 'Age 6' row when all information has been transferred to the grid.

③ Complete each sequence.

Q	AC	DF	GI	JL	___
	AZ	BY	CX	DW	___
	1AA	2BB	3AA	4CC	___

Answers: MO, EV, 5AA.

The skills required for this question type are logical ordering, following patterns and finding links between groups of letters and numbers. The strategy is to look at the links between the first letter of each set and then the next. It's important not to get confused by looking at the sequence of the letters together, but in relation to the other groups of letters. For example, not to look at the relationship between A and C or D and F but to look at the relationship between A and D and then C and F. Here is a worked example with the alphabet to help:

A B C D E F G H I J K L M N O P Q R S T U V W X Y Z

A to D = +3   D to G = +3   G to J = +3
We now know that our first letter must be J +3 = M.

C to F = +3   F to I = +3   I to L = +3
We now know that our second letter must be L + 3 = O.

The answer to the first question then is MO.

> *All of these question types are explained in further detail in the* Bond How to do Verbal Reasoning *book which can be bought or ordered from most bookshops. (See Appendix B for details.)*

Non-verbal Reasoning

Non-verbal reasoning tests look at patterns and shape rather than words and verbal processes. They test whether a child can problem solve, whilst working quickly and accurately, and how effectively they can process information through graphic or pictorial representation. But what does this really mean? Non-verbal reasoning tests can be broken into four sections: Identifying Shapes, Missing Shapes, Rotating Shapes and Coded Shapes.

- Identify shapes and patterns
- Pair up shapes
- Recognise shapes that are similar

- Find a given part within a shape
- Find a missing shape from a pattern
- Find shapes that complete a sequence

Identifying Shapes   **Missing Shapes**

Rotating Shapes   **Coded Shapes**

- Recognise mirror images
- Relate shapes to given nets
- Link nets to cubes

- Code and decode shapes using letters
- Code and decode shapes using numbers
- Apply shape logic

Let's have a look in more detail at each section and understand how you can help your child succeed at non-verbal reasoning.

Identifying shapes

This section develops the visual recognition of shape and pattern. Can your child recognise symbols and shapes that are alike? Can they sort shapes by colour, direction, size and number of sides? Typical identifying shapes questions might include the following examples.

(1) The first two shapes are related in some way. Can you circle the fourth shape that is related to the third in the same way as the second is related to the first?

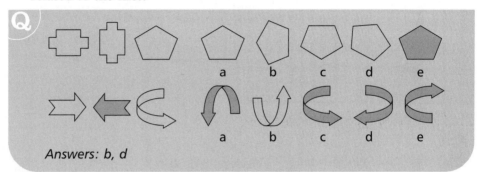

Answers: b, d

The skill required for the type of question is an understanding of what has changed between the first two shapes. Once this connection is made, the same connection can be applied to the next set of shapes.

For example, the second shape has changed colour and is pointing in the opposite direction from the first shape:

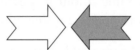

Now we are looking for a changed colour and opposite direction version of this third shape.

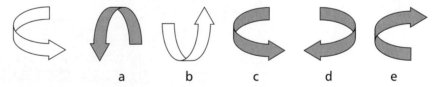

In this example, shape 'a' has changed colour but is not an opposite direction.
Shape b hasn't changed colour and isn't an opposite direction.
Shape c has changed colour but hasn't changed direction.
Shape d has changed colour and it is in an opposite direction.
Shape e has changed colour but is not an opposite direction.

We can now see that shape d is the answer.

The strategy here is to create a logical pattern of questioning for your child to follow.

For example:
- Has the shape turned 90 degrees to the right?
- Has the shape turned upside down?
- Has the shape turned 90 degrees to the left?
- Has the shape changed colour?
- Has the shape grown bigger or smaller?

By using this template it encourages your child to think in a logical and ordered way which will make answering this type of question easier.

(2) Circle the two shapes that are identical.

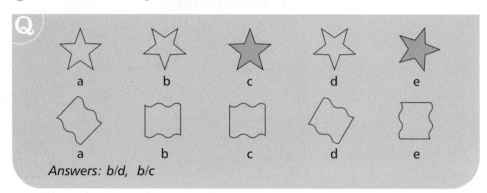

Answers: b/d, b/c

The skill required in this question is the ability to match alike shapes by recognising what selected shapes have in common. The strategy is to take note of the direction, size and colour of the shapes and to exclude any shape that is obviously unrelated. This should then identify the exact match. By working through those facing the same direction, of the same size, of the same colour it is easier to pair up shapes. Working from left to right helps to create a systematic order for this process.

(3) Circle the one odd shape out.

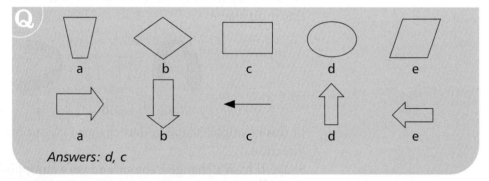

Answers: d, c

The skill tested here is the ability to work out a relationship that links four of the shapes together leaving an odd one out. The strategy required is to first try looking at common areas such as colour, type of shape (all straight edges, has four sides, are based on a circle, etc.) size and direction.

For example, in the first question all shapes have four edges except for the oval, in the second question all shapes are block arrows except for c.

This section develops spatial awareness and understanding of rotation of shape and pattern. Can your child recognise patterns within a pattern? Can they recognise a pattern when it is rotated? Typical missing shapes questions include the following examples.

(1) In which picture is the shape on the left hidden?

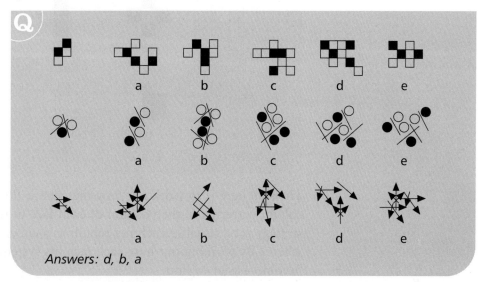

Answers: d, b, a

The skills required here are the ability to recognise shapes (identifying individual parts of a larger shape and being able to find exact matches) and the ability to rotate shapes mentally. The strategy needed is to work from left to right looking for identical elements and this can be easier if the partial shape is broken down further. In question 1 for example:

• Look for two diagonal black squares.

• Check if the two diagonal black squares have white squares directly underneath.

This systematic approach is more effective and quicker than staring at each shape hoping the answer will appear, especially when the shapes might be in a rotated form.

IIII▶ TRY THIS!

It might be helpful for your child to turn the paper so that the pattern is at the same rotation. This can make it easier to recognise the shape they are after.

Rotating Shapes

This section looks at the nets of cubes and how objects look when they are rotated. Here is an example of a typical rotating shape question:

(1) Match the nets with their cubes by writing the letter of the cube under its net.

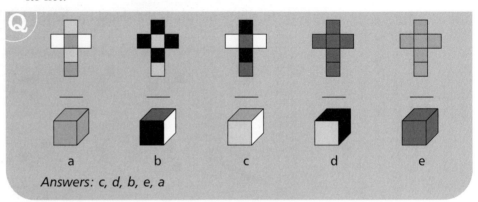

Answers: c, d, b, e, a

The skill here is to work out how the cube will look as a net by considering colour, pattern and the position of each face in relation to each other. The strategy is to visualise each net rebuilt as a cube. Which colour face goes where? By working out how each face fits systematically, the answer becomes easier to find.

> **TRY THIS!**
>
> Encourage your child to use 3D modelling to develop spatial awareness. Building blocks and some of the computer design games like 'Sim City' and 'The Sims' are all helpful for this type of question.

Coded Shapes

This section considers the connection between shapes and letters or shapes and numbers using codes to find relationships. Typical coded shapes questions include the following.

(1) Complete the code for the last shape.

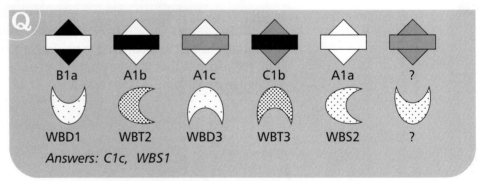

Answers: C1c, WBS1

The skills required are the ability to pair a code with a shape and the ability to then interpret the encoded shape. The strategy here is to work out which code goes with which shape, colour, size or direction. A logical system makes this easier. For example, with the first question we could follow a thought-process like this:

- All shapes have a 1 in the middle.
  The last shape must have a 1 in the middle.

- All shapes with a black background are initially coded B.
  All shapes with a white background are initially coded A.
  All shapes with a grey background are initially coded C.
  This shape has a grey background so must be initially coded C.

- All shapes with a white rectangle are coded a.
  All shapes with a black rectangle are coded b.
  All shapes with a grey rectangle are coded c.
  This shape has a grey rectangle so must be coded c.

The answer must therefore be C1c.

> *All of these question types are explained in further detail in the* Bond How to
> do Non-verbal Reasoning *book which can be bought or ordered from most
> bookshops. (See Appendix B for details.)*

English

11+ English tests cover the elements of reading and writing. They examine how effectively a child can understand and use the English language. But what does this really mean? English tests can be broken into four sections: Comprehension, Spellings, Punctuation and Grammar and Word Choice.

- Read for understanding
- Take answers from a given text
- Understand beyond a given text
- Recognise proverbs and sayings
- Match words and definitions

- Fill in missing letters
- Put words into alphabetical order
- Work out abbreviations
- Recognise spelling mistakes

Comprehension **Spelling**

Punctuation and Grammar **Word Choice**

- Use nouns, verbs, adjectives and adverbs
- Understand contractions and compounds
- Add prefixes and suffixes to roots
- Choose suitable punctuation
- Understand tenses

- Understand homophones and homonyms
- Change singular and plurals
- Choose words to complete a text
- Use conjunctions to create clauses
- Recognise antonyms and synonyms

Let's have a look in more detail at each section and understand how you can help your child succeed at English.

Comprehension

This section is all about reading and understanding information that is given in a text. Is your child a strong reader? Do they pick up written information quickly and efficiently? Some questions require a child to understand common English proverbs and sayings. Here are some examples of comprehension questions based on this short extract from a fairy story.

> Megan was not brave enough to peep from under the duvet. She knew the monster was waiting for her. Megan had called for help but when her brother Ryan had come in, he had teased her, 'There's nothing at the window you silly baby. Look!' He had pulled back the curtain and sure enough, there was nothing there. The wind was making the pear tree branches creak and groan and in a strong squall the tips of the twigs swished against the window frame, but other than that, the night was certainly not the centre stage for monsters and ghosts. Ryan pulled the curtains together and went back to his room laughing, but Megan didn't feel reassured. Eventually, she took a steady breath and appeared from under the bedcover. Clearly against her thin, pink curtains, she could see the silhouette of the monster's spiky, long arms moving about. She could see the sharp pins in the monster's arms and she could hear it moaning her name. It was going to get her. She could hear the monster knocking on the window, trying to get in. Megan screamed.

From *The Monster At My Window* by Michellejoy Hughes

(1) Which one of these statements is true?

Q
A The branches were blown by the rain.
B The twigs touched the window frame.
C There were pears on the tree.
D The leaves creaked and groaned.
Answer: B

HINT

Remind your child that sometimes the same words occur in several places so care is needed to answer the question correctly.

The skill required here is for your child to read the text carefully in order to understand what is written and to look for the answers to the questions. It also requires knowledge of writing styles. The strategy needed is for your child to highlight the main words in the question and then find these words in the extract. When these words are found, your child needs to read the sentence containing the words to understand the context.

(2) Which word could have been used instead of 'silhouette'?

Q
A Noise
B Echo
C Outline
D Darkness
Answer: C

The skill required here is for your child to be able to think beyond the text, to use the clues given in the text to form an answer. The strategy for answering this type of question is to carefully read the text making sure your child understands what it is about. Here is an example using question 2 above:

> she could see the **silhouette** of the monster's spiky, long arms moving about.

A she could see the *noise* of the monster's spiky, long arms moving about.

B she could see the *echo* of the monster's spiky, long arms moving about.

C she could see the *outline* of the monster's spiky, long arms moving about.

D she could see the *darkness* of the monster's spiky, long arms moving about.

We can see that *noise* and *echo* don't make sense, as sound cannot be seen and *darkness* doesn't explain the movement of the monsters' arms.

The only word that makes sense then, is *outline*.

✔ HINT

If your child does not know the answer, they should look at the answers given and reject the ones that are definitely wrong and then decide which of the remaining options seem the most likely. This might include thinking about other stories your child has heard of, or other uses of a word.

IIII▶ TRY THIS!

Word definition is important for this type of question. Quizzes, dictionary games and crosswords will all help to build your child's knowledge. The Schonell Spelling books are also very good for developing word knowledge. (See Appendix B for details.)

③ What is meant by 'in a strong squall the tips of the twigs swished...'?

> **Q**
> A When there was a loud noise, the twigs moved.
> B The twigs were constantly moving.
> C The twigs moved like a hurricane.
> D When the wind blew especially hard, the twigs moved.
> *Answer: D*

The skills required here are a knowledge of words and phrases and the ability to understand the context of words within a text. The strategy for answering this type of question is for your child to decide which of the answers is most likely. Sometimes looking at the smaller words within the text can help. For example, in question 3 the word 'in' is vital as it suggests a connection with the 'strong squall'. It is only when there is a strong squall that the twigs move and so answers B and C are automatically disregarded. We could see this question as a logic table:

	ACTION	RESPONSE
	In a strong squall	**the twigs move**
A	When there's a loud noise	the twigs move
B	All of the time	the twigs move
C	All of the time	the twigs move like a hurricane
D	When there is strong wind	the twigs move

There has to be a specific action to make the twigs move.
    A Can noise move twigs?
    B No specific action here.
    C No specific action here.
    D Strong wind could make the twigs move.

From this we know the answer is D.

Spelling

This section is all about spellings and word choice. Does your child have a high spelling age? Do they easily remember spelling 'rules'? How do they perform at their school spelling tests? Here are some typical spelling related questions:

(1) In these sentences there are either no spelling mistakes or one spelling mistake. Underline the sentences that do have spelling mistakes.

> Q A Charlotte was not aware of the darkness that engulfed her.
> B She could see only the bright light in the distance.
> C Foecusing on the light she carefully got up.
> D Holding onto the wall for suport, she moved slowly.
> *Answer: C, D*

✓ HINT

Knowing the rules of spelling such as 'i before e except after c' and 'plural f becomes a ves' are invaluable.

The skill required in these questions is an ability to recognise incorrect and correct spellings of words. Sometimes it will be an individual word that is given and sometimes a complete sentence so careful reading is needed.

The strategy here is to gain spelling knowledge and to recognise common errors in spelling.

> **IIII▶ TRY THIS!**
>
> Encourage your child to write out variations of a tricky word in their own handwriting. This can sometimes help them to visualise the correct answer. Spelling books such as the Schonell range are so useful for this type of question. (See Appendix B for details.)

(2) If these words were put in reverse alphabetical order, which word would come third?

> Q Abhorrent, Abolition, Adhesive, Abolished, Adhered
> *Answer: Abolition*

The skills required here are knowledge of alphabetical order and the ability to look methodically at words. Sometimes the questions will ask for reverse alphabetical order so each question needs to be read carefully. The strategy here is to work logically and carefully. Encourage your child to write out the alphabet first if it isn't included on the exam paper. Working from left to right, your child needs to consider each letter in turn to work out the correct order. One successful method is to rewrite each word directly below each other to make the letter ordering easier. For example, here is the original order of the words:

	1	2	3	4	5	6	7	8	9
1	A	B	H	O	R	R	E	N	T
2	A	B	O	L	I	T	I	O	N
3	A	D	H	E	S	I	V	E	
4	A	B	O	L	I	S	H	E	D
5	A	D	H	E	R	E	D		

- Column 1 shows us that all words begin with A so we move to column 2.

- Column 2 shows three words have a second letter B and two words have a D. As B comes before D in the alphabet, we should first look at the three words with a B in rows 1, 2 and 4. (abhorrent, abolition, abolished).

- In rows 1, 2 and 4 column 3 shows the letters H and O. As H comes before O in the alphabet, we know our first word is ABHORRENT. Now look at the other two 'AB' words in rows 2 and 4.

- Columns 4 and 5 are identical for these words but in column 6 we have T and an S. S comes before T in the alphabet, so we now know that our second word is ABOLISHED and the third word is ABOLITION.

- Looking next at the two AD words in rows 3 and 5, we can see they are identical until we reach column 5 when we have an S and R. R comes before S in the alphabet, so we know our fourth word is ADHERED and our fifth word is ADHESIVE.

✔ HINT

Sometimes the question will ask for alphabetical order and sometimes reverse alphabetical order, so encourage your child to read the question very carefully.

The reordered table, showing the five words in alphabetical order, will then look like this:

	1	2	3	4	5	6	7	8	9
1	A	B	H	O	R	R	E	N	T
2	A	B	O	L	I	S	H	E	D
3	A	B	O	L	I	T	I	O	N
4	A	D	H	E	R	E	D		
5	A	D	H	E	S	I	V	E	

If we go back to the question it asks, 'If these words were in reverse alphabetical order, which would come third?' Because we have these words in alphabetical order, all we need to do is work from the bottom up to find the third word. We now know that our answer is Abolition.

(3) What is the correct abbreviation for the royal society that prevents cruelty to animals?

> **Q** A RSPCB   B RSPCA   C RSPCC   D RSCA   E SCAPE
> *Answer: B*

The skills required here are a knowledge of abbreviations and an understanding of how abbreviations work. The strategy is to be aware of how we can abbreviate words and to think of what words might be represented by the abbreviations.

> **▶ TRY THIS!**
>
> The *Bond How to do 11+ English* book offers help with abbreviations and acronyms whilst the Bond English papers give children plenty of practical experience of using and understanding these terms. The *Bond No Nonsense English* range also offers practice on abbreviations and acronyms. (See Appendix B for details.)

Punctuation and Grammar

This section is all about understanding syntax, sentence and word structure. Does your child write correct sentences? Do they understand how and when to use punctuation? Do they understand the classes of words such as nouns, verbs and prepositions? Can they add suffixes and prefixes to root words? Here are some examples of typical punctuation and grammar questions.

(1) Look at the word 'side' in these sentences and then give the class of how the word is used (e.g. as a noun, verb, adverb, adjective, preposition).

> **Q** A She knocked on the side door.   _____
> B The crab waddled sideways.   _____
> C The whole side was badly damaged. _____
> D The book was at the side of the telephone._____
> E He could side with either of them.   _____
> *Answer: adjective, adverb, noun, preposition, verb*

The skill required here is knowledge of word class and how a word can change its classification depending on the context of the word. The strategy needed is for your child to be clear on the classifications and their meanings. Encourage them to look at a sentence and to decide what role each word has. Using a logical system of questions like this can be useful:

- Where is the noun – the main thing or object?
- Where is the adjective that describes this noun?
- Where is the verb – the doing word, the action?
- Where is the adverb that describes this verb?
- Is there a preposition that describes the place?

② Rewrite this passage correctly, adding each new conversation on a new line and looking carefully at punctuation.

> jess and josh decided that theyd go to the zoo at chester arent you ready yet shouted their friend john no but well only be a minute replied jess youd better hurry or well miss the bus john said jess and josh rushed downstairs to grab their coats
>
> *Answer:*
> *Jess and Josh decided that they'd go to the zoo at Chester.*
> *"Aren't you ready yet?" shouted their friend John.*
> *"No! But we'll only be a minute," replied Jess.*
> *"You'd better hurry or we'll miss the bus," John said.*
> *Jess and Josh rushed downstairs to grab their coats.*

HINT

Remind your child that speech marks need to go before the spoken words begin and immediately after they have finished.

The skills required here are an awareness of punctuation and how it should be used and a methodical eye to read the text carefully. The strategy is to read the selected text underlining all words that need capital letters, placing slashes at the points where each line should end and marking where the speech marks should be. The text then needs to be copied placing apostrophes, commas, full stops, question marks and exclamation marks in all of the right places. Highlighting the text first before copying it out means that sentences end at the correct places and capital letters are identified before mistakes can be made.

③ Underline the root of these words.

> Judgement, Incorrectly, Rewired, Impossible, Misinformed
> *Answers: Judge, Correct, Wire, Possible, Inform*

HINT

Encourage your child to make sure every letter underlined is just the root word as a slightly too enthusiastic line can render the answer incorrect.

The skill required here is knowledge of how root words, prefixes and suffixes work. The strategy is to look carefully at whether the word given has just a prefix or suffix or whether it has both.

▐▶ TRY THIS!

A useful game to play with your child is to start with a small word and add a letter at a time to see how long the word will grow. For example, the word 'at' can become 'hat' and then 'hate' and then 'hated' and then 'heated' and then 'cheated'. When they can understand that a root word can grow and change, it makes prefix and suffix work so much easier for them to understand.

An extension to this game is to give your child a word and get them to add a prefix or suffix or preferably both. For example, the word 'write' can become 'written' and then 'rewritten'. All of these games are great for in the car/waiting room/at the table and they really help to develop word craft.

---

④ Underline any of the following sentences that are in the past tense.

> A Phil would be going to the gym.
> B Jon is sitting on the stool.
> C Rob was here.
> D Caleb had eaten his tea.
> *Answer: C, D*

The skill required is an awareness of how words change within the context of a sentence. Your child needs to be aware of the past, present and future tenses of words. The strategy for answering this type of question is to create a logical thinking pattern:

- Past tense: Has it happened already?
- Present tense: Is it happening now?
- Future tense: Has it yet to happen?

By looking at each statement and applying this thinking pattern, it is easier to work out whether a statement is written in the past, present or future tense. Here is an example using question 4A:

Phil would be going to the gym.

Past tense: Has Phil already gone to the gym?   *(Phil had been to the gym.)*

Present tense: Is Phil at the gym now?   *(Phil is at the gym.)*

Future tense: Is Phil going to go to the gym?   *(Phil will/would be going to the gym.)*

From working through these questions, we now know that this statement is in the future tense.

> **TRY THIS!**
>
> A useful game to play is to create a sentence and encourage your child to change the sentence into another time frame. Begin with simple sentences such as 'The dog is here' which can become for example: 'The dog was here' or 'The dog will be here'.

Word Choice

This section is about how each word can work and which word is best for a particular job. Can your child understand singular and plural? Can they find words to fit into sentences and can they join phrases together to make their writing more interesting? Here are some typical word choice questions.

(1) Underline the correct word in each sentence.

> **Q**   A The women swim / swims towards the edge of the pool.
>
> B The stables were full of horse / horses.
>
> C They came across the herd of deers / deer.
>
> D It was so quiet! Where were all the man / men?
>
> *Answers: swim, horses, deer, men.*

The skills required here are knowledge of plural and singular word forms and how some words change when they are pluralised. The strategy needed is for your child to consider the whole sentence and to select the word that makes sense. Some questions that might help your child to reach the answer could be:

- Does the sentence make reference to a singular noun or more than one?

- What is the plural of words such as deer, ox, fish and buffalo?

- Is the word needed one that has just an 's' on the end or does the spelling need to change?

② Add a suitable connective word to join these clauses together.

Q A She couldn't see the book _____ it was on the table.

B The dog was barking _____ it wanted to go outside.

C Vicky cried _____ her cat was sick.

D Alex was so tired _____ he'd been playing football.

Answers: although/because/when/as/but, because/as, because/when/as, because/when/as
(Any of these examples are suitable.)

The skill required here is an understanding of how clauses can be connected using connective words. Words such as 'because, although, but, when, and' etc. have an important job in making simple phrases complex.

The strategy needed is for your child to read both clauses and to understand how they relate to each other. It is then easier to choose a suitable word that reflects this relationship. For example, consider the range of possible connective words with the first pair of clauses:

She couldn't see the book _____ it was on the table.

    She couldn't see the book *and* it was on the table.
    She couldn't see the book *but* it was on the table.
    She couldn't see the book *when* it was on the table.
    She couldn't see the book *although* it was on the table.
    She couldn't see the book *because* it was on the table.
    She couldn't see the book *as* it was on the table.

From these examples, we can see that 'and' doesn't fit but all of the other words sound correct and make sensible sentences. Encourage your child to see how the sentence changes depending upon the connective word used.

③ Complete the table using words from the passage.

Q The day was cold and wet. James left the house wishing he was still in his warm and dry bed. He hated going to school when the weather was so horrible. There again, James hated going to school whether it was nice or nasty weather! His school tie was rubbing against his chin as James bent down to tie his laces.

Pair of homophones		Pair of homonyms		Pair of antonyms	

Answers: (others are possible)

Pair of homophones		Pair of homonyms		Pair of antonyms	
weather	whether	tie	tie	wet	dry

The skills required here are a knowledge of word types and the ability to apply this knowledge to a given text. The strategy needed is to read the text carefully highlighting all examples of homophones/homonyms/antonyms etc.

Make sure your child is comfortable with what these terms mean. See below for useful definitions.

✓ HINT

Definitions

Homophones	Words that sound the same but have a different meaning and are usually spelt differently.	to plane *wood*. to fly a *plane*.
Homonyms	Words that are spelt the same, sound the same but have different meanings.	*their* clothes. *over* there. *they're* brothers.
Antonyms	Words that are opposites.	*wet/dry, cold/hot*
Synonyms	Words that have a similar meaning.	*wet/damp, cold/chilly*

All of these question types are explained in further detail in the Bond How to do 11+ English *book which can be bought or ordered from most bookshops. (See Appendix B for details.)*

Maths

11+ Maths tests cover a spectrum of maths principles and concepts. They examine how effectively a child can understand and manipulate numbers. 11+ Maths tests can be broken into four sections: Graphic Data, Shape and Size, Number Equations and Number Logic.

- Use graphs, charts, tables and decision trees
- Understand co-ordinates and compass points
- Work out scale and dimension
- Understand conversions

- Recognise shape, symmetry and rotation
- Understand vertices, faces and edges
- Find size, perimeter and volume
- Describe angles of movement

Graphic Data | **Shape and Size**

Number Equations | **Number Logic**

- Use division and multiplication
- Understand multiples of numbers
- Use addition and subtraction
- Work out fractions and percentages
- Recognise equations
- Use prime, square and cube numbers

- Apply number logic
- Use negative and positive numbers
- Understand number lines
- Make number squares
- Understand probability and ratio
- Use mean, mode, median and range

Let's have a look in more detail at each section and understand how you can help your child succeed at maths.

Graphic Data

This section covers the use of co-ordinates, compass points and the elements of scale and dimension. Can your child understand conversions? Can they use decision trees and read tables, graphs and charts? Typical questions in the area of graphic data include the following.

1 Look at this timetable and answer the questions.

	High St	Wood End	The Bank	Lodge Rd	Terminus
Bus A	09:14	09:20	09:50	10:03	10:15
Bus B	10:00	10:06	- - -	10:30	10:42
Bus C	11:20	- - -	11:45	11:58	12:10

A How long does Bus A take to get from High St. to the Terminus?

B How long does it take from Lodge Rd to the Terminus?

C What is the quickest time from Wood End to Lodge Road?

Answers: 1hr 1minute, 12 minutes, 24 minutes.

The skill required is to make deductions from the data given and a general awareness of subtraction and addition is also useful. The strategy needed is to look at what the question is actually asking. For example, in question C, your child is trying to find the quickest time from one place to another so it is not sufficient to use any bus but to make comparisons with one against another.

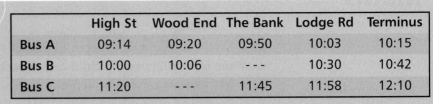

TRY THIS!

Try to encourage your child to read maps, tables, timetables and graphs. Get them involved in real, or imagined, travel arrangements by asking them to find the quickest/shortest route from A to B using a train or bus timetable. Even reading the salt or calorie content on a box of breakfast cereal can help sharpen a child's ability to find information efficiently.

2 Look at this grid and answer the following questions.

```
        A   B   C   D
N    1  B   Q   B   B
↑    2  Q           X
     3          Q   F
     4  Q   B   Q   B
```

KEY

X = treasure
B = bomb
Q = quicksand
F = forest

A At what co-ordinate can the treasure be found?

B In what direction is the forest from the treasure?

C What is the co-ordinate for the bomb furthest west?

Answers: D2, South (S), A1

The skill here is to recognise how the grid reflects the key, how the co-ordinates work and where the compass points are. The strategy needed is for your child to understand that each co-ordinate is mapping an item described in the key. Knowing how to relate the compass point with the grid and key, and understanding that co-ordinates are read across the horizontal and then down the vertical, means information can be retrieved accurately and quickly.

③ Look at the following chart and answer the questions.

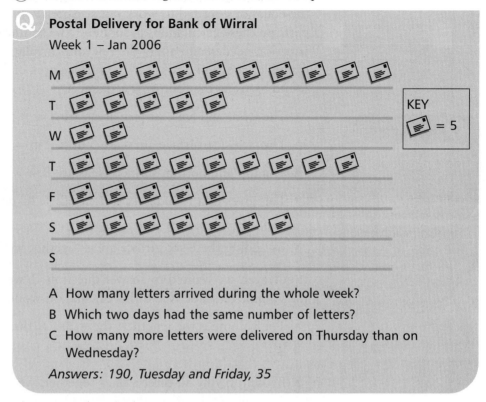

Q

Postal Delivery for Bank of Wirral
Week 1 – Jan 2006

KEY

✉ = 5

A How many letters arrived during the whole week?

B Which two days had the same number of letters?

C How many more letters were delivered on Thursday than on Wednesday?

Answers: 190, Tuesday and Friday, 35

The skills required here are the ability to make comparisons between data and an awareness of basic calculation. The strategy needed is to first recognise what the key means and then apply it to make sense of the chart. Your child needs to be able to associate M T W T F S S with the title (Week 1) to understand that this is about deliveries of letters on a day-by-day basis. They also need to recognise that each symbol represents five letters. Once this is understood it is important to carefully read each question to find exactly what information is needed.

Shape and Size

This section looks at shape and its symmetry and rotation. It considers the elements of a shape and how knowledge of faces, sides and angles can help calculate size and volume. Typical questions in the shape and size section include the following.

① Look at the following shapes and then answer the questions.

HINT

Shape and size terms:
Area: the surface size
Edge: the side
Face: the flat surface
Volume: the internal size
Perimeter: the outer boundary
Vertices: the corners

Q

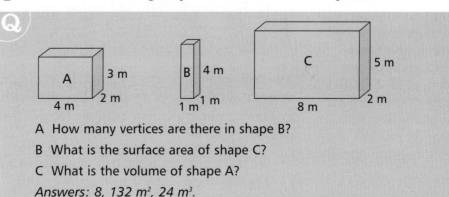

A How many vertices are there in shape B?

B What is the surface area of shape C?

C What is the volume of shape A?

Answers: 8, 132 m², 24 m³.

The skills required are an understanding of the terms used, knowledge of the equations needed to work out size/area/volume etc., and the ability to perform these calculations accurately. The strategy here is to recognise the equation needed and apply the relevant calculations to each question. For example, question B asks for the surface area of shape C, which can be found by using the following sequence:

- The front and back surface areas are $8\,m \times 5\,m = 40\,m^2$ each.
- The two side surface areas are $5\,m \times 2\,m = 10\,m^2$ each.
- The top and bottom surface areas are $8\,m \times 2\,m = 16\,m^2$ each.
- This gives us a total of six surfaces $(2 \times 40\,m^2) + (2 \times 10\,m^2) + (2 \times 16\,m^2)$.
- By adding these six surface areas together we have the answer of $132\,m^2$.

If however, we wanted to answer question C, we would need to work out the volume of shape A and this calculation would be as follows:

- The volume is the length × the width × the depth.
- $4 \times 3 \times 2$
- By multiplying all three values together, we have the answer of $24\,m^3$.

 Which of these shapes has at least one pair of parallel sides?

> A regular pentagon
> B rhombus
> C trapezium
> D isosceles triangle
> E regular hexagon
> *Answers: B, C, E*

The skill required is a knowledge of shape and an understanding of parallel lines. The strategy is to recognise which shapes have parallel lines and which do not.

 In the parallelogram below, angle x measures 70°. What is the size of angle y?

Answer: 110°

The skill required here is a knowledge of angles and the calculations needed to work out the size of an angle. The strategy is to create a logical sequence in working out angles. For example for this question it is helpful to consider questions such as:

- What relationship is the pair of angles to a circle?
  The two angles make a semi-circle or 180°.
- If one angle is 70° we can take this from 180° to leave the answer.
  The answer must be 110°.

 HINT

Make sure your child knows how to work out each measurement. Revising multiplication will help.

 HINT

If they are unsure, encourage your child to sketch out the shapes so they can see where the parallel lines are. Reinforcing the number of sides for each shape can help, as can helping your child to learn and recall the different types of triangles.

The y angle is the same as the angle next to x and these two angles together make a semi-circle.

Number Equations

This section looks at the fundamental calculations in maths: multiplication, division, addition and subtraction. It considers fractions, percentages, root numbers and basic equations. Some typical questions using number equations include the following.

① Jason goes to Scouts, (70p a week). He plays in the orchestra, (£1.20 a week), he plays football twice a week, (£1.10 each time), he goes to Chinese school, (£16.80 every four weeks) and he goes to drama, (75p a week).

> **Q**
> A What is the total cost for Jason each week?
> B If Jason does these activities for 46 weeks of the year, how much would it cost at the end of the year?
> C If Jason pays for the year in advance, he will get a reduction of 10%. How much would he pay now for the year?
> *Answers: £9.05, £416.30, £374.67*

The skill here is the ability to perform addition, division, subtraction and multiplication as well as understanding percentages.

The strategy is to break this question down into manageable chunks. Encourage your child to set out the initial sums into an easy to read format and then to work out each calculation methodically. For example:

A	B	C
£1.10 × 2 = £2.20 (Football) + £16.80 ÷ 4 = £4.20 (Chinese School) + £1.20 (Orchestra) + £0.75 (Drama) + £0.70 (Scouts) £9.05	£9.05 × 46 £416.30	Hint: *He gets 10% discount, so he pays 90% of the total year's cost.* 1 £416.30 ÷ 100 = £4.1630 2 £4.1630 × 90 = £374.67

② Underline the odd one out.

> **Q**
> A 9   16   25   81   101
> B 0.1   0.25   0.5   0.75   1
> C 25%   50%   75%   80%   100%
> *Answers: 101, 0.1, 80%*

The skills here are recognising square numbers, decimals and percentages and finding a link that makes one answer the odd one out. The strategy needed is to find the link between the numbers. In the first question it is looking at square numbers and in the second and third answers, looking for the odd numbers in the middle of $\frac{1}{4}$, $\frac{1}{2}$, $\frac{3}{4}$, 1. For example:

25%   50%   75%   80%   100%

- We can see there is a link as 50% is half of 100%

- Another link is that 25% is half of 50% and a quarter of 100%

- If we look at halves and quarters being a possible link, we can see that 80% is the odd one out as it does not follow this pattern.

▶ TRY THIS!

Encourage your child to think in a logical way when trying to find the connection, for example:
- Are the numbers squared?
- Do they follow an addition or subtraction pattern?
- Are they in the same multiplication table?
- Do they follow a common pattern in fraction or decimal form?

(3) Complete the grid.

	$3 + x$	$5 - x$	$7x$	$12 \div x$	$x + x + x$
$x = 2$					
$x = 3$					

Answers:

	$3 + x$	$5 - x$	$7x$	$12 \div x$	$x + x + x$
$x = 2$	5	3	14	6	6
$x = 3$	6	2	21	4	9

The skill required here is a recognition of an equation where x represents a given number and to carry out calculations using $x =$ to complete a grid. The strategy is first to understand the grid and then to replace x with the numbers given in each equation. Encourage your child to use a logical thinking pattern to fulfil each criterion. For example:

If $x = 2$ then:	If $x = 3$ then:
$3 + x =$	$3 + x =$
$3 + 2 = 5$	$3 + 3 = 6$ and so on...

▶ TRY THIS!

Any games that use calculations are useful for these types of questions. Sudoku books and the Yahtzi number board game are especially popular, although BEAM make a range of maths games that are really popular with pupils (see www.beam.co.uk). Even polishing up the times tables can help in an exam when every second counts.

Number Logic

This section looks at negative and positive numbers, number squares, number lines and the manipulation of statistics through averages and range. Some typical number logic questions include the following examples.

(1) What are the missing numbers in each number square?

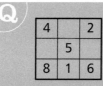

4		2
	5	
8	1	6

	18	
6	10	14
16		12

6	18	21
12	24	9

Answers: 9, 3, 7   8, 4, 2   27, 3, 15

The skill here is recognising how a number square works and then calculating the missing numbers by fulfilling the rules of the number square.

The strategy is to work out what each line needs to add up to and then to work out what numbers are missing. Here is an example for the first number square:

4		2
	5	
8	1	6

1 I need to look for a complete row and there are three here, the two diagonals and the bottom row.

2 The total of each completed row adds up to 15.

3 I now need to make sure all rows add up to 15.

4 My answers are 9, 3 and 7.

(2) Cathy Robins gives her four children pocket money each week. She gives out a total sum of £20 and divides the money in relation to the ages of the four children. Rachael is 16, Alex is 14, Louise is 12 and Nicholas is 10 and the pocket money is given out 1:2:3:4 with the largest portion to the eldest child and the smallest portion to the youngest child.

Q
A How much pocket money does Rachael get?
B How much pocket money does Alex get?
C How much pocket money does Louise get?
D How much money does Nicholas get?
E What is the average amount?
Answers: £8, £6, £4, £2, £5

The skills required are an understanding of how ratio and averages work and the ability to apply a calculation to find the correct answers. The strategy here is to divide the total sum of money between the four ratio amounts. For example:

1 Find the total of the ratio amounts: $4 + 3 + 2 + 1 = 10$.

2 Divide the total sum of money by the ratio total: $£20 ÷ 10 = 2$.

3 Multiply this by each ratio number to give the total pocket money per

child:

$4 \times £2 = 8$

$3 \times £2 = 6$

$2 \times £2 = 4$

$1 \times £2 = 2$

4 Add up the money and divide by the number of children to find the average.

£20 $(8 + 6 + 4 + 2) \div 4 = £5$.

(3) Look at these number lines and calculate the numbers that the arrows point to.

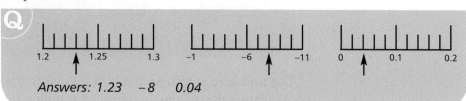

Answers: 1.23 −8 0.04

✓ HINT

Encourage your child to check between two consecutive points (not just assuming the beginning point is 0) and remind them that number lines can move in any direction between positive and negative numbers.

The skill required is to recognise the increments on a number line and to then find a given point. The strategy needed is to establish what the starting and ending numbers are and the incremental steps along the number line. Here is an example of the last number line above:

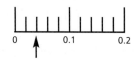

1 There are five steps between 0 and 0.1.

2 There must be 0.02 between each step (0.10 ÷ 5 steps = 0.02).

3 The arrow must be pointing to 0.04.

⫸ TRY THIS!

Encourage your child to read measurements whenever possible whether from a ruler, a thermometer or scales. It is also useful for your child to understand how scale can move in small or large stages, perhaps showing them the large difference between a petrol gauge in a car or the small weight difference between 10 g and 15 g of sultanas.

All of these question types are explained in further detail in the Bond How to do 11+ Maths *book which can be bought or ordered from most bookshops. (See Appendix B for details.)*

11+ Frequently Asked Questions

Q *How is the 11+ different to other school exams?*

National exams such as SATs are part of the government framework for education. GCSEs are a cornerstone of secondary school learning and although not compulsory, they are internationally recognised qualifications that are offered in most schools. The 11+ exam is part of the secondary school selection process for schools that select by academic ability.

Q *How fierce is competition for the 11+?*

There are always more pupils applying for grammar schools than there are places available, sometimes as many as 10 pupils for every one place and so competition is fierce. When a school has an admissions policy based on the 11+ results only, those with the highest results take the places.

Q *Why is it so hard to find out information about the 11+?*

Since the 1970s there has been a political move away from selective school processes to state school comprehensive systems. For this reason, less schools and LEAs are using the 11+ selection system. Many schools within 11+ LEAs are reluctant to prepare for the 11+ and in some cases they would prefer to give the minimum amount of information to parents.

Q *Can past papers be bought for practice?*

For the LEAs who commission an exam board to write the 11+ paper, it is not usually possible to beg, borrow or steal past exam papers. What you can get hold of are general example papers written by the exam boards, which can be bought from bookshops. For those schools that set their own papers, they will often send out copies of past papers, as will schools that sit the Common Entrance Exam.

Q *My child is bright at many subjects but struggles at Maths/English – what can I do to help them?*

The Bond Placement Tests in this book will help to identify where the problem areas are and will suggest which books your child needs to strengthen a weak area. Each book in the series is carefully graded to ensure steady progress is made and the answer booklets make it easy for parents to check accuracy.

Q *My child was ill for their SATs and we don't know what level they are at. What should we do?*

Have a word with your child's class teacher and see what level they think your child is working at. The different methods of assessing your child may not be complete but as long as you have at least the results from the Bond Placement Tests plus one other area of comparison, (reading age, SATs results or school/teacher report would be especially useful) you should be able to gain some idea of where your child is up to. Some schools prefer not to inform parents of where their child is up to in their SATs, so again, use the results from the Bond Placement Tests plus at least one other form of assessment.

Q *My child is bright and capable but they are very slow to work questions out. Does this mean they are going to fail the 11+?*

The Bond system uses timed papers and following the books will ensure your child becomes used to working within a time frame. See the Bond *How to do* range for ideas of how to improve the techniques your child uses and then gradually shorten the length of time given for each paper.

Q *My child is top of the year but it is not an academic school. How can I tell how bright my child is compared to pupils in other schools?*

The Bond Placement Tests in the middle of this book will help you to assess your child against a standard and to find out where your child is in terms of the 11+ needs and requirements.

Q *If I put my child in for the 11+ it means I will lose my position for the next best school. It is a huge risk to take so is it worth it?*

There is no guarantee that any child will or will not pass the 11+ but by using the Bond Placement Tests you will be able to tell where your child is up to. You can then make a more informed decision based on how they have done and how much time you have to follow the Bond system until the 11+ exam is due. If your child has an above national level in SATs and reading age and the school has provided feedback that your child is working on the highest level of work (top set, top table or the more advanced books) it would suggest that your child is working at 11+ standard already. If the results of the Bond Placement Tests and school/other sources of information are showing similar results and you have a year until the actual 11+ exam, it would be a good indication of a strong candidate. If, however, your child has a below average reading age, they are average in their school progress, the results of the Bond Placement Tests suggest your child needs to work at the level 2 books in English and maths and you have only a couple of months until the 11+ exam day, you would be taking a far greater risk in your expectations.

Q *If I am undecided about entering my child for the 11+ is there any other benefit to following the Bond system or is it purely geared for the 11+ exam?*

The Bond system covers English, maths, verbal and non-verbal reasoning. The English and maths are matched to the National Curriculum and many parents choose to follow the system in order to prepare their child for school based SATs, which often determine the sets that secondary schools place pupils in. A thorough grounding in English and maths will never be a waste of time or money. In fact, preparing your child for secondary school is a very sensible use of time and money and the Bond system provides a cost effective and systematic way of doing so. Verbal and non-verbal reasoning develop skills of logic, systematic thinking and problem solving. These topics don't directly follow the National Curriculum or any school-based subjects but they develop transferable skills that can be used across the curriculum, widening the core skills of any pupil.

Q *If my child fails the 11+ can they retake it?*

No. Sorry, but it is a one and only opportunity although some schools will recognise the 12+ exam. This is similar to the 11+ but is taken a year later. It is ideal for pupils who are in the Middle School system or pupils who wish to enter the selective secondary school beyond year 7, but who have not sat the 11+ exam. Of course those of you in a LEA that does not use the 11+ will have the opportunity of sitting an 11+ style entrance exam for as many schools as you are applying for.

Q *Can I buy my position in a school if my child fails the 11+?*

Sorry, but if a school says it goes by academic achievements only via the 11+ exam, money won't alter that policy. Some schools do accept pupils who fit other criteria such as music or sporting achievements, but these schools would state in their prospectus that the entrance examination is only part of their selection process.

Q *My child has educational/physical/emotional needs. Isn't this a disadvantage?*

Individual schools should all have a policy on fair examination opportunities for all children. The test papers and test environment should fully cater for your child whether it is for large print, extra time or whatever your child needs to be given a fair attempt of the paper. Make sure you notify schools in advance so that they have time to prepare.

Q *Will my child need to sit an interview as well as completing the 11+?*

For many grammar and private schools there are no interviews. Parents are notified when the results are through, if their child has a place. There are other schools that invite just the child along for an interview and schools where both the child and the parent/s are interviewed. If your child is invited for an interview, they will often be asked to bring along schoolbooks and sometimes certificates or awards from 'out of school' activities. This needs to be selective so do include your child's latest music, dance, sporting award or newspaper cuttings of events your child has taken part in, but don't take along every piece of art work your child has created, or certificates older than a couple of years. (You are rightly proud of their 'Little Ducklings Pre-School Swimming Certificate for Improvement', but a secondary school will be more impressed to see that your child has been swimming on a regular basis for nine years, as this shows dedication and perseverance).

Q *How should my child prepare for an interview?*

Make sure your child is confident about the activities they have done and explain how these might help them in secondary school. For example, 'Playing in the primary school football team has helped me to be focused and to work well with others,' or 'Playing the flute in the orchestra has helped me to be confident'. The interviewer is looking for pupils who will best suit the school environment. Read the school prospectus to see what they value. Do they mention sports teams, debating societies, music activities, drama groups, reading schemes, travel opportunities or church events? What has your child done that links with this (avid member of the village library) or demonstrates a transferable skill (reading shows a thirst for knowledge and keen mind)?

Q *Can my child sit the 11+ for private and grammar schools?*

Yes. Your child can sit the 11+ in their primary school if you are in an 11+ LEA and then the 11+ exam in private schools. If your school is not in an 11+ LEA you could sit several 11+ exams in selective schools.

Q *Is it possible to pass the 11+ without having a private tutor?*

Yes. Some pupils will pass the 11+ without ever having taken any 11+ tuition or having seen practice papers. Other pupils will work through a couple of practice papers, some will work through a year or more of books at home and some will have private tutors. As with most things, if you are prepared for something you can usually deal better with it. It is important to remember that every child is different and what might suit one child won't suit another. Whatever system you choose, don't be afraid to change it if it isn't working effectively for your child.

Q *So why should I bother following any system of 11+ help for my child?*

Quite simply, the more opportunity your child has for prior practise and preparation, the easier the exam will be and the more chance your child will have of passing. They are building up confidence and experience and when your child is up against the clock, preparation can make all the difference.

Q *Why is Bond preferable to other 11+ systems?*

Bond offers a complete package of books and test papers that make up a tried and tested route through the 11+. The Bond Placement Tests in this book are a vital key to assessing your child and they work in harmony with the rest of the series. Bond doesn't have full colour quiz books with stickers, games and gimmicks because that isn't what the 11+ exam is like. Instead it offers a cost effective, thorough and concise action plan that, used in conjunction with this guide, will offer all of the support and information you and your child need.

In a recent interview, Michellejoy said:

❧ *I didn't start writing for Bond and therefore begin to use their system. I was using every book in the series well before. I have tried all of the major books and series out there and believe me, between the computer programs, downloadable papers and the countless books in the 11+ market, that's a lot of material. Some are excellent, some are appalling and many are neither one nor the other. I've tried them all but came to Bond through experience and have never looked back. Bond is my choice because the information is complete and thorough, pupils enjoy the series, parents can easily follow the system and can track the progress of their child. The books are affordable and offer excellent value for money and wherever you are in the country the information is suitable for all 11+ and selective school exams. I recommend the Bond series to parents because it is what I use myself and my results show for it. The books don't have gimmicks, stars, stickers, cartoons or other distractions but offer a solid, thorough, complete learning programme.* ❧

Checklist for Step 1 Success

☐ I know what the 11+ test is

☐ I know when my LEA 11+ test is and what is tested

☐ I understand what verbal reasoning is about

☐ I understand what non-verbal reasoning is about

☐ I understand what English is about

☐ I understand what maths is about

☐ I'm ready to assess my child

I still need to find out more about...

....

....

....

Bond Placement
TESTS

- Verbal Reasoning
- English
- Maths
- Non-verbal Reasoning

These pull-out papers may be photocopied for personal use only.

Good Techniques

1 Always use a pencil so that changes can be made.
2 Read each question thoroughly so that you do not misunderstand what you have to do.
3 If there is an example given, make sure you understand it.
4 Work logically from left to right to create a systematic order.
5 If you don't know an answer, move on and if you have time at the end come back to it.
6 It is always better to make a logical 'guess' than to leave a blank space.

VERBAL REASONING

LEVEL 1

The alphabet is to help you with the first two questions.

A B C D E F G H I J K L M N O P Q R S T U V W X Y Z

Fill in the gaps in the following sequences.

1   A35 is to B40 as C45 is to _____   **2**   29A is to 31B as 33C is to _____   `2`

Fill in the missing number in each sequence.

3   1   2   4   7   ___   16   **4**   40   36   ___   28   24   20   `2`

Complete these sums.

5 $4 + 6 + 8 = 3 \times$ _____   **6** $44 \div 11 = 2 \times$ _____   `2`

Underline one word in the bracket to make each expression correct.

7   Boy is to girl as man is to (woman, person, adult)   `1`

8   Mountain is to high as valley is to (fast, slow, low)   `1`

Underline the two words that are made from the same letters.

9   mate meet term atom team   **10**   site stem mast seat teas   `2`

`10`
TOTAL LEVEL 1

LEVEL 2

Complete the following sentences by selecting one word from each group of words given in the brackets. Underline the words selected.

1   The old man (smiled, yawned, laughed) because he was (tired, worried, ill) and wanted to go to (hospital, bed, shops).   `1`

2   She turned on the (lights, curtains, towels) as it was getting (light, dark, sunny).   `1`

Underline the pair of words most similar in meaning.

3   young, old brief, short good, bad   **4**   talk, speak read, story bed, time   `2`

Underline the two words, one from each group, that go together to form a new word. The word in the first group always comes first.

5   (birth, help, cradle) (less, more, much)   **6**   (let, come, in) (room, doors, stairs)   `2`

Find the three-letter word, that can be added to the letters in capitals to make a new word that will make sense. Write the word in the space.

Example: The footballer SCO a goal. (SCORED) Answer: red

7   It STED to rain.   _____   `1`

8   We FOLED the path to the sea.   _____   `1`

CONTINUE TO THE NEXT PAGE

Find a letter that will end the first word and begin the second.

Example: CA _ AP Answer: T (cat tap)

9 MOS____IME   **10** RIC____OME

2

10
TOTAL
LEVEL 2

LEVEL 3

Underline the word that has the same meaning as the word in capital letters.

1	ABBREVIATE	disown	repeat	lengthen	shorten	delay
2	PURSUE	run	follow	quarrel	fight	hurt
3	PARDON	save	forgive	fight	imprison	hate

1

1

1

Find a word that can be put in front of each of the following words to make new compound words.

EXAMPLE: day set burn shine   Answer: SUN (Sunday, sunset, sunburn, sunshine)

4	cream	hockey	skating	berg	_____
5	root	load	stairs	turn	_____
6	house	gage	fingers	grocer	_____

1

1

1

Find and underline the two words that need to change place for the sentence to make sense.

EXAMPLE: The <u>trees</u> were resting beneath the <u>elephants</u>.

7 I pot the flower turned over.

8 It is wilting and the flowers are hot.

9 We must wait and sit until it is our turn.

1

1

1

Underline the word that cannot be made from the letters of the word in capital letters.

10	FORGIVEN	grief	given	grove	green	giver
11	SERVICING	vices	singe	serve	giver	grins
12	SUNSHINE	shine	shins	shuns	sheen	sushi

1

1

1

Give the next number in the following sequences.

13 1   20   2   19   ____   **14** 319   428   537   646   ____

15 1   8   27   63   ____

2

1

15
TOTAL
LEVEL 3

LEVEL 4

Underline two words, one from each group, which are opposite in meaning.

EXAMPLE: (<u>reduce</u>, sale, market)   (bargain, <u>increase</u>, shopping)

1 (annoy, discomfort, reward)   (punishment, painless, distress)

2 (slave, expensive, free)   (work, dear, enslave)

3 (cause, perfect, mistake)   (error, flawed, flat)

1

1

1

PLEASE TURN OVER

The Parents' Guide to the 11+
© Michellejoy Hughes, Nelson Thornes Ltd 2006

Write these words in alphabetical order.

4   precise   precious   pretty   present   prettier

_____ `1`

5   graphic   graph   gracious   graphite   graceful

_____ `1`

Write the four-letter word hidden at the end of one word and the beginning of the next word.
The order of the letters must not be changed.

EXAMPLE: He liked fis<u>h and</u> chips = hand

6   The house was surrounded by a circular drive. _____ `1`

7   They have rye bread for breakfast.   _____ `1`

8   So dad rescued the kitten from the tree.   _____ `1`

The alphabet is to help you with the next two questions.

A B C D E F G H I J K L M N O P Q R S T U V W X Y Z

The word HOLDER is written in code as IPMEFS. Encode these words using the same code.

9   LOSE   _____   **10**   HOLE   _____ `2`

If A=1, B=3, C=5, D=6, E=10 and F=12, what is the value of the following words if the letters are added together?

11   FACE   _____   **12**   FADED   _____ `2`

Jenny, Julie, Jemima, Jo and Justine are all learning to dance. Jenny loves Jazz and Ballet. Julie hates Ballet but loves everything else. Jemima loves Classical, Tap and Ballet. Jo doesn't like Jazz, Classical and Folk. Justine likes Tap best but she also likes Folk.

13   Which is the most popular dance?_____ `1`

14   Who likes the most dances?   _____ `1`

15   Who likes Classical dance?   _____ `1`

`15`
TOTAL
LEVEL 4

VERBAL REASONING RESULTS		DATE:		
	LEVEL 1	LEVEL 2	LEVEL 3	LEVEL 4
SCORE				
Total Mark For Verbal Reasoning Test:				

ENGLISH

LEVEL 1

*Circle the **pronouns** in each sentence.*

1   I love cheese on toast.   **2**   Where has she gone? `2`

CONTINUE TO THE NEXT PAGE

*With a line, match each word with its **definition**.*

3 Foul   a baby horse

     Daffodil   a cold blooded animal

     Foal   to break the rules

     Reptile   a spring flower   `1`

4 Several   someone who serves

     Nostril   more than a few but not all

     Server   clouds of gas and small bits of solid material

     Smoke   opening at the end of your nose   `1`

Underline the root in each word.

5 unclearly   **6** impatiently   `2`

Underline the correct word in brackets to make sense of each sentence.

7 The sea (was / were) peaceful and calm. **8** The baby (drank / drinked) the milk. `2`

Change these words into the past tense.

9 Help _____   **10** Do _____   `2`

                                                            `10`
TOTAL LEVEL 1

LEVEL 2

Put these verbs in the present tense.

1 drank _____   **2** crept _____   `2`

Add the missing apostrophe to these nouns.

3 Daniels rabbit.   **4** The milkmans overalls   `2`

Write the letter that matches the expression with its meaning.

5 **a** a wet blanket   **b** full of beans   **c** a bookworm

     filled with energy and high spirits __

     a miserable person   __

     a keen reader   __   `1`

6 **a** pins and needles   **b** horse play   **c** with flying colours

     rough and boisterous   __

     great success   __

     cramp in the limbs   __   `1`

PLEASE TURN OVER

The Parents' Guide to the 11+
© Michellejoy Hughes, Nelson Thornes Ltd 2006

Read this short extract and then fill in the table with two examples of each word group used in the passage.

> The brown bull looked at Sompiti. Deciding that she was not that interesting, he carried on his slow chewing of the grass but he never took his big, dark eyes away from her. Sompiti carefully stepped back, not wanting to make the bull angry. She wished more than anything that she had not chosen to wear her long, red dress. Perhaps it was not true that red made bulls angry but she wasn't going to hang around just in case!

7	NOUN		
8	VERB		
9	ADVERB		
10	ADJECTIVE		

1
1
1
1
10
TOTAL
LEVEL 2

LEVEL 3

Read this poem and then answer the following questions.

> Autumn Time
>
> Golden yellow butter pouring through the window,
> White fluffy sheep, scampering through the sky,
> The brightest paint box blue, what a lovely backdrop,
> That's what I see with my artist's eye.
>
> Green frothy bubbles bend and squash under my feet,
> Gifts from the trees, crunchy crisp and dry,
> Trees left with bony arms that wave goodbye to me,
> That's what I see with my artist's eye.
>
> *Michellejoy Hughes*

1 How does the poet refer to the clouds?

_____

2 What do you think the 'golden yellow butter' is?

_____

3 What phrase describes the grass?

_____

4 Why has the tree got waving bony arms?

_____

5 What do you like best about this poem and why?

_____

_____

1
1
1
1

CONTINUE TO THE NEXT PAGE

Add a connective word to join the phrases together.

6   I need that book _____ it is too high for me to reach.   `1`

7   Jon is my best friend _____ we play cricket together.   `1`

8   The children were noisy _____ the teacher walked in.   `1`

9   Make three compound words from these words.

      out   in   with   let   ring   side   house   green

_____   _____   _____   `1`

Underline the correctly spelt words.

10   The fish were (silvery / silvary) and (slippery / slippary).   `1`

11   The (libary / library) was well (equipt / equipped).   `1`

12   He (might / mite) buy a (magazine / magasine).   `1`

13   She (tried / tryed) to (separate / seperate) them.   `1`

Add both a prefix and a suffix to each word to make one new word.

14   mind _____   **15**   equal _____   `2`

`15`
TOTAL LEVEL 3

LEVEL 4

Write a short definition for each of these words.

1   lubricate _____   `1`

2   abbreviate _____   `1`

3   resolve _____   `1`

4–8   *Circle all of the words that are spelt incorrectly in this passage.*

> The casle was old and bleak. It had a mot running around it but the
> stagnant water was filthy and green. She bit her tonge as she looked at
> the half derelict building and wanderd what had purswaded her father to
> buy it.

`5`

Read this passage and then fill in the table.

> I can do maths but I cannot do English. I've never read a book let alone seen
> a stage play although we did one scene of Macbeth last term. Best of all I like
> PE because I get to play football every Wednesday. My team kit is red and
> white and always looks good! Worst of all is science because I cannot
> understand it; too many things to remember and my class are not that good.

9	Proper nouns		
10	Collective nouns		
11	Pair of antonyms	and	and
12	Pair of homophones	and	and

`1` `1` `1` `1`

PLEASE TURN OVER

The Parents' Guide to the 11+
© Michellejoy Hughes, Nelson Thornes Ltd 2006

13 Write six synonyms for the word 'said'.

_____   _____   _____

_____   _____   _____

1

14 *Underline the reported speech.*

"Are you ready yet?" asked Tom.   Tom asked "Are you ready yet?"

Tom had asked if he was ready yet.   Tom asked him if he was ready.

1

15 *Rewrite this text with the correct punctuation.*

> there are many people who say why bother with exams theyre aware of
> the importance of qualifications but cant understand why one bad day
> could ruin the rest of your future I would agree in part to this but say a
> well prepared pupil will always fare better than one who is relying on luck

_____

_____

_____

_____

_____

_____

1

15
TOTAL
LEVEL 4

ENGLISH RESULTS			DATE:	
	LEVEL 1	LEVEL 2	LEVEL 3	LEVEL 4
SCORE				
Total Mark For English Test:				

MATHS

LEVEL 1

A dinner lady puts four rows of pasties in the oven. There are six pasties on each of the four rows.

1 How many pasties does she bake?   _____

1

2 Write one thousand and seven in figures.   _____

1

Put a < or a > sign in each of the spaces.

3 (7 + 2) ____ 8   (2 + 6) ____ 7

4 (5 + 4) ____ 10   (3 + 5) ____ 6

1
1

What are the answers to these number sentences?

5 13 + 27 = _____   43 + 36 = _____

6 82 − 63 = _____   96 − 33 = _____

1
1

CONTINUE TO THE NEXT PAGE

Underline the correct answer.

7   56 ÷ 8 = (6 7 8 9)   **8**   7 × 7 = (42 48 49 56)

9   81 ÷ 9 = (7 8 9 10)   **10**   4 × 12 = (36 45 48 50)

LEVEL 2

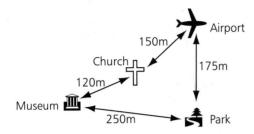

1   How many metres is it from the Church to the Park, stopping at the Museum? _____

2   How many metres is it from the Church to the Park, stopping at the Airport?   _____

Fill in the gaps in this multiplication table.

3
4
5
6

×	2	__	4
__	10	15	__
10	__	__	__
__	__	45	__

7   *Name these shapes:*

A   _____

B   _____

C   _____

8   *Circle the numbers divisible by 5.*

     4   5   12   15   45   55   97   120

Mark the lines of symmetry on these shapes.

9 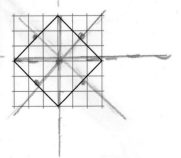   **10**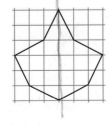

The Parents' Guide to the 11+
© Michellejoy Hughes, Nelson Thornes Ltd 2006

LEVEL 3

Fill in the missing numbers in each line.

1   2.5   4   5.5   7   ___   ___

2   ___   38   34   30   26   ___

3   33   ___   39   42   ___   48

What are the answers to these number sentences?

4   468 × 7 = _____

5   452 × 4 = _____

6   372 × 8 = _____

7   987 × 9 = _____

Underline the correct answer.

8   10 × 1000 = 1000   10 000   101 000   1010

9   10 ÷ 100 = 0.1   0.01   0.001   1

10   0.472 × 10 = 4.72   47.2   0.0472   472

I need to wrap these tins of biscuits up and each tin shows how much wrapping paper I need.

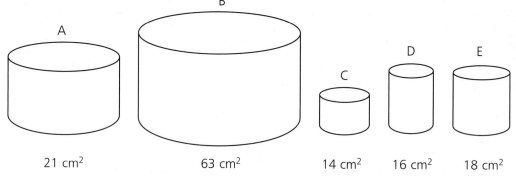

A   B   C   D   E

21 cm²   63 cm²   14 cm²   16 cm²   18 cm²

11   Tin _____ requires three times the amount of paper as tin _____ .

12   Tin _____ requires half as much again as tin _____ .

13   If I wrapped up tins C, D and E I would need _____ cm² of paper.

14   There are 297 children in Year 6. For every 14 girls there are 13 boys.

There are _____ boys and ____ girls in Year 6.

15   There are 50 teachers in the school. For every two male teachers there are three female teachers.

There are ___ male teachers and ___ female teachers.

LEVEL 4

Underline the correct answer in each line.

1   10 − 1.99 =   9.11   8.01   11.99   9.01

2   2.7 × 200 =   5.4   540   54.00   0.54

3 $\frac{1}{2} + \frac{3}{4}$ = $1\frac{1}{2}$ $\frac{3}{4}$ 2 $1\frac{1}{4}$

CONTINUE TO THE NEXT PAGE

Look at these shapes and then fill in the table.

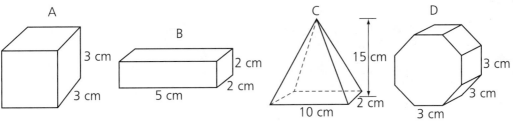

A 3 cm 3 cm

B 5 cm 2 cm 2 cm

C 15 cm 10 cm 2 cm

D 3 cm 3 cm 3 cm

		A	B	C	D
4	number of edges	12	12	8	24
5	number of vertices	8	8	5	16
6	number of faces	6	6	5	10
7	surface area				
8	volume				

Complete the following table.

9	Wholesale Price	£18.75		£5.13	£196.50		93p
10	Retail Price	£23.50	£70.20		£235.25	£13.50	£1.12
11	Profit		£11.35	97p		£2.19	19p

Write these decimals as fractions.

12 3.125 _____

13 7.625 _____

14 4.05 _____

15 9.075 _____

1

1

1

1

1

1

1

1

2

2

15
TOTAL
LEVEL 4

MATHS RESULTS		DATE:		
	LEVEL 1	LEVEL 2	LEVEL 3	LEVEL 4
SCORE				
Total Mark For Maths Test:				

NON-VERBAL REASONING

LEVEL 1

Put a circle round the odd one out on both lines.

1

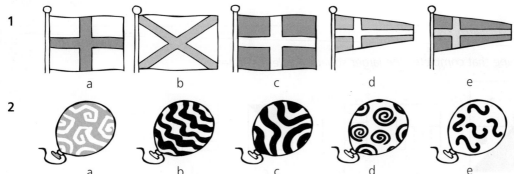

a   b   c   d   e

2

a   b   c   d   e

1

1

PLEASE TURN OVER

K

Circle the picture on the right, which is a reflection of the picture on the left of the dotted mirror lines.

3

a   b   c   d   e

4

a   b   c   d   e

Draw the rest of these shapes as they would be if reflected in the mirror.

5

6

Circle the odd shape out.

7

a   b   c   d   e

8

a   b   c   d   e

The shape on the left is the same as which one on the right?

9

a   b   c   d   e

10

a   b   c   d   e

LEVEL 2

Choose the shape that completes the larger square. Circle the letter.

1

a   b   c   d   e

CONTINUE TO THE NEXT PAGE

1

1

2

1

1

1

1

1

10
TOTAL
LEVEL 1

1

2

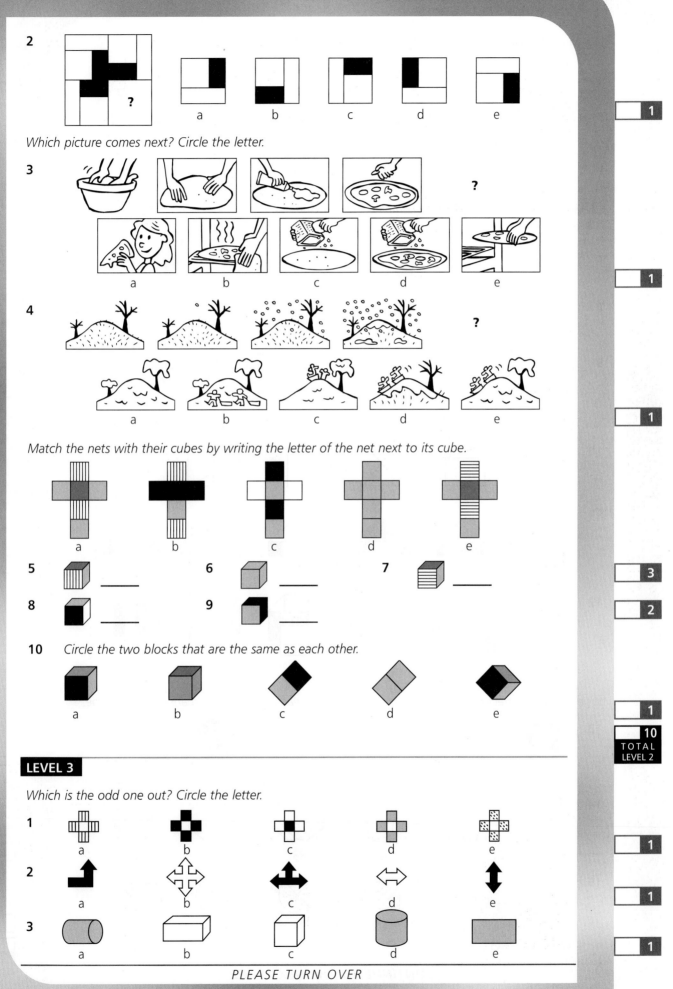

a b c d e

Which picture comes next? Circle the letter.

3

a b c d e

4

a b c d e

Match the nets with their cubes by writing the letter of the net next to its cube.

a b c d e

5 _____ **6** _____ **7** _____

8 _____ **9** _____

10 Circle the two blocks that are the same as each other.

a b c d e

1

1

1

3

2

1

10
TOTAL
LEVEL 2

LEVEL 3

Which is the odd one out? Circle the letter.

1
a b c d e

2
a b c d e

3
a b c d e

1

1

1

PLEASE TURN OVER

The Parents' Guide to the 11+
© Michellejoy Hughes, Nelson Thornes Ltd 2006

Which one comes next?

4 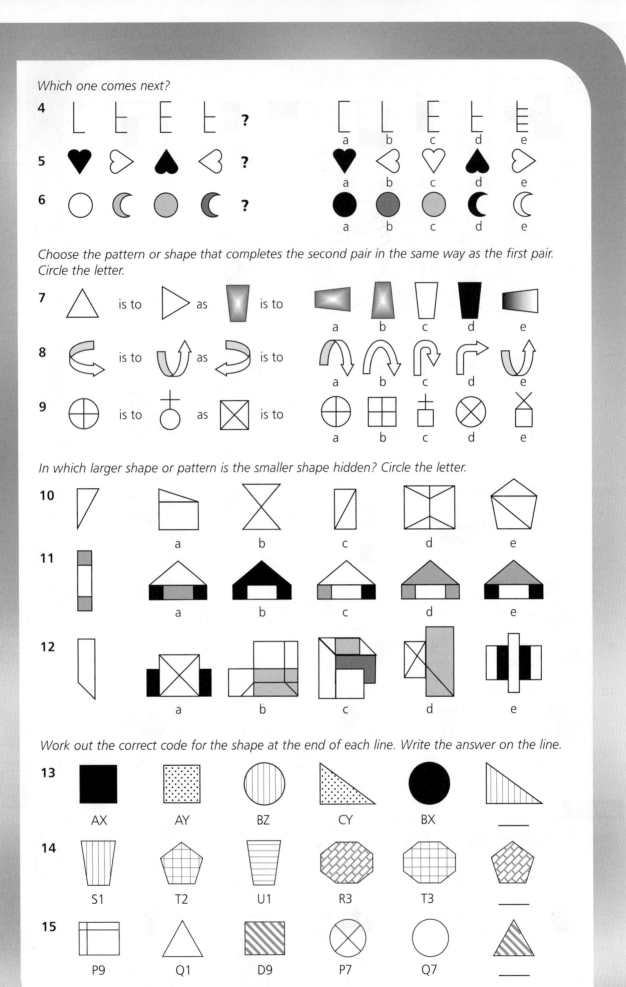 ⌐ ⊦ ⊦ ⊦ **?**   ⌐ ⌐ ⊦ ⊦ ⊦
                                          a b c d e

5 ♥ ▷ ▲ ♡ **?**   ♥ ♡ ♡ ♠ ♡
                    a b c d e

6 ○ ☾ ● ☾ **?**   ● ● ● ☾ ☾
                    a b c d e

Choose the pattern or shape that completes the second pair in the same way as the first pair. Circle the letter.

7 △ is to ▷ as ▯ is to   a b c d e

8 ⊂ is to ∪ as ⊃ is to   a b c d e

9 ⊕ is to ☿ as ⊠ is to   ⊕ ⊞ ☐ ⊗ ⊗
                          a b c d e

In which larger shape or pattern is the smaller shape hidden? Circle the letter.

10
   a b c d e

11
   a b c d e

12
   a b c d e

Work out the correct code for the shape at the end of each line. Write the answer on the line.

13   AX   AY   BZ   CY   BX   ____

14   S1   T2   U1   R3   T3   ____

15   P9   Q1   D9   P7   Q7   ____

CONTINUE TO THE NEXT PAGE

1
1
1
1
1
1
1
1
1
1
1
1
15
TOTAL
LEVEL 3

Which cube could not be made from the given net? Circle the letter.

1

a   b   c   d   e

1

2

a   b   c   d   e

1

Work out the correct code for the shape at the end of each line. Write the answer on the line.

3

T12   W14   T16   W12   Z16   ___

1

4

M3   MS4   MV3   MV4   MS5   ___

1

5

NB   BN   GN   BG   NN   ___

1

Which is the odd one out? Circle the letter.

6

a   b   c   d   e   f

1

7

a   b   c   d   e   f

1

8

a   b   c   d   e   f

1

The Parents' Guide to the 11+
© Michellejoy Hughes, Nelson Thornes Ltd 2006

Which shape or pattern completes the bigger pattern? Circle the letter.

9

a   b   c   d   e

10

a   b   c   d   e

11

a   b   c   d   e

Compare the two shapes on the left. Which other shape goes with this pair? Circle the letter.

12

a   b   c   d   e

13

a   b   c   d   e

Compare the first two shapes. Find another shape that makes a second pair. Circle the letter.

14  is to as is to

a   b   c   d   e

15  is to as is to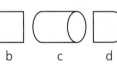

a   b   c   d   e

NON-VERBAL REASONING RESULTS		DATE:		
	LEVEL 1	LEVEL 2	LEVEL 3	LEVEL 4
SCORE				
Total Mark For Non-Verbal Reasoning Test:				

STEP 2

Assess Your Child

❝ *Doesn't every parent think that their own child is a genius? How do I really tell how bright my child is? When I asked the school if my child was suitable for taking the 11+ the teacher said that she didn't believe in the 11+ and would therefore refuse to answer the question. I wish there was another way of assessing my child...* ❞

❝ *My daughter goes to a village school. She is top of her year but then there is only one class in Year 6. She did well with her SATs but so did most of her class. How can I judge how bright she is compared to other children of her age? How can I decide whether it is worth us pursuing the 11+ route into secondary school?* ❞

2

Build Up a Picture of Your Child's Ability

Deciding whether to enter your child for the 11+ exam is a difficult decision that shouldn't be taken until you are fully informed of your child's progress and ability. Here are some key sources of information to gather, that will help with this decision making process.

The Bond Placement Tests

Look at the results from the Bond Placement Tests, which will give an indication of where your child is up to at present. Is there sufficient time for your child to work through to the 11+ level books? Does your child have a spelling age that is at least equal to their real age?

School Report

How is your child performing academically at school? What is the assessment of your child's teacher?

SATs Results

How did your child perform in their last SATs tests? What are their predicted results for the next SATs?

Assess Your Child For The 11+

Reading Age

Is your child advanced in their reading age? Are they proficient at reading for understanding?

Logic Games

Does your child perform well at crosswords, wordsearches, logic games or quizzes? Do they enjoy computer games that require tactical thinking or fast, accurate reactions?

Parental Assessment

How well do you think your child is performing? Do you think your child is academic, quick to learn, fast but accurate in their learning?

No one piece of information can determine your child's ability, but a combination can give you a good indication of how your child might perform in the 11+ examination.

The Bond Placement Tests

The importance of the Bond Placement Tests is to highlight the level your child is at in the four 11+ subjects. This can be considered in terms of the time left to study and the level your child has achieved. Following the step-by-step plans will help make the most of the time available and will suggest the best course of action for your child to follow, in order to give them the best possible preparation for the 11+ exam.

SATs Results

These results show how well your child is performing compared to a national average. The 11+ exam is to determine the top performing pupils to select for grammar and independent school entry. A child who is average or below average in their SATs results is less likely to perform well in their 11+ exam. By the end of Year 6 the SATs expectation is for your child to have reached Level 4 in maths, English and science.

School Report

Your child's teacher and the school report can offer an insight into how your child is likely to perform. Is your child above average in maths and English? Does your child's school have a good academic reputation? How does the school year compare in terms of ability? You might have a child who is doing reasonably well but in another year they would be top, so they may well be more than capable of passing the 11+. Sadly the opposite is also true and your child might be top in the school but compared to the national average, they may be average or even lower than average.

Reading Age

One question to ask the school or to check on the school report is your child's reading age. As with children who have a high spelling age, a good reader with a high reading age is likely to find the 11+ easier than a child who struggles with reading. Fluent reading and understanding is important in a timed test so your child will ideally have an above average reading age. Check in *Bond How To Do 11+ English* for advice and suggested book lists to help with your child's reading (see Appendix B for details).

Logic Games

Does your child enjoy problem solving, crosswords, puzzles and logic games? Are they good at jigsaws, sliding puzzles and mathematical games? All of these are a good indication of a child's ability to grasp ideas of logic and problem solving and are invaluable in the verbal reasoning and non-verbal reasoning 11+ tests.

Parental Assessment

Don't forget that you know your child and their capabilities. Do you really feel they are able to pass the 11+ and do all the indications point to a child who is above average and likely to do well?

Realistic Expectations

Passing the 11+ isn't about fluking it or being lucky on the day. It is a sifting system to separate children by their academic ability. Tutoring your child is useful in giving them self-confidence and strengthening their weak areas, but it is important to be realistic. If your child is clearly not capable of the 11+ without an awful lot of extra help, you may be able to push them to a certain extent, but how much time do you have and will they ever reach the standard required? It's also important to remember that passing the 11+ is only the start of it. If they should scrape through, how will they cope in an academic school that will push their pupils on a constant basis? Could you and your child cope with this on a daily basis for the next five, six, seven years? That is a lot of pressure for a teenager to be under and they may end up gaining far fewer or lower graded academic qualifications than the child who works at their own natural pace and succeeds in a less pressured school environment. Every parent wants the best for their child, but what is best for your child may not necessarily be the 11+ and a grammar school education.

Set The Four Bond Placement Tests

Q *Why are the Bond Placement Tests useful?*

The Bond Placement Tests included in this book are a vital stage in assessing your child. The results of these tests can help you decide what level your child is at and what books they need to progress in time for their 11+ exam. These tests can help you to decide whether it is best to let your child sit the 11+ exam or not, and can help to highlight areas of weakness.

Q *When should my child sit the Bond Placement Tests?*

Although these tests can be used at any time, the best time would be between 18 and 12 months before the 11+ exam takes place. This leaves you with optimum time for preparing your child, but however long you have before the exam, it is worth completing these tests.

Q *What if my child is sitting both the grammar school and private school exams?*

The Bond Placement Tests are suitable for all children whether you are considering a grammar school or private school. You will need to check what subjects your schools use in the 11+ exam and then use the corresponding tests provided here.

Q *Does my child need to sit all four tests?*

The Bond Placement Tests are suitable for wherever you live as different LEAs use different tests. You will need to check what subjects your LEA or individual school is using and then use the corresponding tests provided here. Remember that English and maths underpin the verbal reasoning 11+ exams, so a good overall knowledge of these subjects will be needed even if your LEA just does the verbal reasoning paper.

Q *What is the difference between multiple-choice and standard format exams?*

Some 11+ exams are in standard format, meaning that children will write their answers beside the questions on their 11+ exam paper. The multiple-choice paper has a separate answer booklet and children mark their answers out of a choice of four or five options. The questions are not necessarily different, just the marking system. The tests here are in standard format but are to be used by all children regardless of what your area does. It is recommended that all children follow a standard format system of learning until they are ready for test papers and at that level, you can then introduce the multiple-choice paper. This is because children need to understand how to do the questions first and then how to fill in the answer booklets as a final stage in their 11+ learning.

Q *Where can I buy the Bond Placement Tests?*

The Bond Placement Tests are only available with this book. These tests have been created to form a solid structure on which to assess children. Each level corresponds with a *Bond Assessment Papers* workbook level, providing a seamless crossover from placement test to workbook progression. The types of questions in the tests are the same as any of the 11+ study systems and the same type as the actual 11+ exams that your child will sit. They work as an integrated part of the Bond system, which provides maximum support.

Q *Are the Bond Placement Tests just for the 11+?*

Although they are perfect for 11+ assessment, the maths and English tests are ideal for all children as they follow the National Curriculum guidelines that schools use and will ultimately help in preparation for school SATs exams.

Q *Does my child need to do all of the Bond Placement Tests in one go?*

Allow your child 30 minutes of uninterrupted time to complete each test. There are four tests in total, which can be divided into four separate sessions of 30 minutes, or two sessions of 1 hour.

Q *Should I help my child or read through the paper with them?*

It is really important that your child works through these tests on their own. Explain to your child that they are to do their best and not to worry about any questions they cannot complete, but to do as much as they can, making a guess at anything they are not sure of. Because the tests are timed, you might want to give them a 'half time' and a 'five minutes before the end' reminder.

Q *What is the spelling test for?*

The spelling test (see page 56) is another useful assessment of your child's ability. Ideally your child will have a spelling age the same or better than their actual age. *The Schonell Essential Spelling Books* are recommended if your child has a lower spelling age (see Appendix B for details).

The answers to the tests are at the back of this book (see Appendix C), so when your child has completed the tests, mark their answers, record their results in the results chart (see page 59) and then find out how to interpret them and create a Personal Learning Plan in Step 3.

Bond Placement Tests Checklist

My child will need to sit the following Bond Placement Tests:

☐ Maths   ☐ English

☐ Verbal reasoning   ☐ Non-verbal reasoning

In order to do their best, your child will need the following:

1 ☐ Pencil

2 ☐ Eraser

3 ☐ Pencil sharpener

4 ☐ Flat surface to work on, e.g. table or desk

5 ☐ A well lit, quiet area to work

6 ☐ Spare paper for any rough working

7 ☐ A watch or clock to check timing

8 ☐ The right time (You would be amazed how much the results can differ when the same child takes the test late at night in front of the television when they are hungry, thirsty, tired and grumpy!)

Find the Spelling Age

Another useful test for grading your child is a spelling test. It is worthwhile finding the spelling age of your child at the same time as taking the Bond Placement Tests and then every four months to check what progress has been made. The spelling test can be used for all primary school ages and is a useful guide as to how your child is progressing. The words selected here have been chosen to represent a cross-selection of graded high frequency words.

In order to find your child's spelling age, read out this list of 50 words for your child to write down. Repeat each word twice in a clear voice but don't over pronounce the words. Allow your child a few seconds to write each word down, but if they are struggling, ask them to spell the word as they think it is.

cat	cut	rat	bin
dad	pen	with	from
yard	good	dream	yearly
mind	sooner	call	while
headache	mistake	height	large
island	bought	lamb	wealth
strayed	bargain	decrease	policy
valleys	library	museum	style
cushion	similar	equally	slippery
earlier	leisure	mortgage	generous
especially	immediate	separate	difficult
apparatus	equipped	politician	committee
permanent	difference		

When the test is over, compare the spellings with the words here.
Allocate your child 1 mark for each correctly spelt word.
Don't allow marks or half marks for 'almost right' words.

1 Add up the total out of 50.

2 Double the score.

3 Divide this number by 10.

4 Add on 5.

Example 1:

Charlotte is 9 years and 8 months.
Charlotte has a score of 27. Her spelling age is:

(Double the total score) $27 \times 2 = 54$

(Divide this number by 10) $54 \div 10 = 5.4$

(Add 5 to this number) $5.4 + 5 = 10.4$

Her spelling age is 10 years and 4 months, which is higher than her real age by 8 months. Because Charlotte's score is higher than the average (her real age), it would indicate an advantage in English and verbal reasoning.

Example 2:

Kang is 10 years and 4 months.
Kang has a score of 19. His spelling age is:

(Double the total score) $19 \times 2 = 38$

(Divide this number by 10) $38 \div 10 = 3.8$

(Add 5 to this number) $3.8 + 5 = 8.8$

His spelling age is 8 years and 8 months which is lower than his real age by 1 year and 8 months. Because Kang's score is lower than average it would indicate a disadvantage in English and verbal reasoning. As the 11+ exam for Kang would take place soon, it is unlikely for there to be sufficient time for Kang to work at spellings in order for him to perform well in the 11+ exam.

HINT

No one test result can be seen as a definitive guide, but all the separate parts add weight to the whole. If, in Example 2, Tom is a bright child who has a high grade on the Bond Placement Tests but has a problem with spelling, it would not necessarily mean he would fail the 11+ exam, he may just struggle on the spelling elements of the exam. The spelling test is a good indicator when used in conjunction with other forms of assessment.

✝ TRY THIS!

To help improve your child's spelling age, the *Schonell* series is recommended, as this develops spellings and word knowledge and includes an *Essential Spelling List* of the most common words suitable for children sitting the 11+. Bond's *How to do 11+ English* develops word awareness and is again ideal for 11+ pupils and their spelling ability. (See Appendix B for details.)

When your child has completed the Bond Placement Tests, use the answer section in Appendix C to mark the papers. You then need to fill in the results chart (see page 59) to help you decide where your child is at and what help they need. Here is an example of how to fill in and interpret the results:

Jem is in Year 5 and he sits the placement tests. His scores are as follows:

Maths Level 1 – 10/10	English Level 1 – 10/10
Maths Level 2 – 9/10	English Level 2 – 10/10
Maths Level 3 – 8/15	English Level 3 – 10/15
Maths Level 4 – 4/15	English Level 4 – 7/15
VR Level 1 – 10/10	Non-VR Level 1 – 10/10
VR Level 2 – 10/10	Non-VR Level 2 – 10/10
VR Level 3 – 8/15	Non-VR Level 3 – 12/15
VR Level 4 – 2/15	Non-VR Level 4 – 10/15

Spelling Age = 11 years 9 months

• To find the percentage – double the TOTAL score for each subject.

Age: 9yrs 11 months		Spelling age: 11yrs 9 months		
SCORES	Maths	English	VR	Non-VR
Level 1	10	10	10	10
Level 2	9	10	10	10
Level 3	8	10	8	12
Level 4	4	7	2	10
TOTAL	31	37	30	42
%	62%	74%	60%	84%
Months to 11+ exam: 12				

We can see that Jem is strong on his non-verbal reasoning and English and weaker at his maths and verbal reasoning. He is only really starting to struggle at Level 4 in his English, but at Level 3 for his maths and verbal reasoning. Jem does have a spelling age that is higher than his actual age, which does indicate an advantage in English.

Here is the results chart for your child's results.

Age:		Spelling age:		
SCORES	Maths	English	VR	Non-VR
Level 1				
Level 2				
Level 3				
Level 4				
TOTAL				
%				
Months to 11+ exam:				

In order to interpret your child's results, you need to confirm the relevant 11+ subjects for your area and then get an initial sense of what the results show in these subjects. If you have decided to put your child forward for the 11+ exam, move on to Step 3 and learn how to create a personal action plan based on this results chart.

Checklist for Step 2 Success

☐ I know what the 11+ test consists of for the school(s) of my choice

☐ I've checked my child's current / predicted SATs scores

☐ I've checked my child's spelling age

☐ I've checked my child's reading age from their school

☐ I've consulted my child's school reports

☐ I've spoken with my child's school teacher

☐ I've set my child the Bond Placement Tests

☐ I've recorded the results of the Bond Placement Tests

☐ I've made a decision on my child sitting the 11+ exam

☐ I'm ready to move on to preparation for the exam

I still need to find out more about ....

....

....

....

STEP 3

Prepare for the Exam

> ❝When is it a good time to start preparing for the
> 11+ test? My child is in Year 4 – is it too early to think
> about it yet? Should I be doing something now to get
> her ready and if so, what? ❞
>
> ❝I know I've left it late as my child is sitting
> the 11+ in a few weeks. What can I do to help him? I
> don't know where to start and there are so many 11+
> workbooks in the shops that I really have no idea where
> to begin. I don't want to waste any more time but I
> need a quick, effective system. ❞

By now you will have assessed your child and decided whether you are going to enter your child for the 11+ exam. Ideally, you will have a clear 12 months from your preparation time to the actual date of the 11+ exam. If you have longer, congratulations, as you will have time to take it more gradually and apply less pressure on your child. If you have less than 12 months, you will need to decide how much you have to do with your child in the time between now and the exam.

In order to make optimum use of the time you have available, you need to draw up a regular plan of study for your child in the form of a personal learning plan. This will show you which books you need to cover, and the amount of time your child has to work through them.

Let's look back at Jem and his results chart.

Age: *9yrs 11 months*		Spelling age: *11yrs 9 months*		
SCORES	Maths	English	VR	Non-VR
Level 1	*10*	*10*	*10*	*10*
Level 2	*9*	*10*	*10*	*10*
Level 3	*8*	*10*	*8*	*12*
Level 4	*4*	*7*	*2*	*10*
TOTAL	*31*	*37*	*30*	*42*
%	62%	74%	60%	84%
Months to 11+ exam: *12*				

We know that Jem is strong with his non-verbal reasoning and English, as he only starts to struggle at Level 4 for these subjects. We also know that he is weaker in maths and verbal reasoning, as his scores start to dip at Level 3. We now need to know which subjects the 11+ exam he is taking consists of; in this case, a combination of maths and English in a standard format. He can therefore put the verbal and non-verbal reasoning to one side and concentrate on improving his maths and English.

In his English Placement Test, Jem achieved a score of over 85% in Levels 1, 2 and 3 but his score dropped below 85% at Level 4. Because of this Jem would start on the *Bond Assessment Papers in English 10-11+ years*, as there is obviously work at Level 4 that Jem needs to understand. When he has completed the Level 4 book he can continue to the *Bond Assessment Papers in English 11+-12+*, which is an extension book for ages 10–11+.

In his maths Placement Test, Jem achieved a score of over 85% in his Level 1 and 2 papers, but his score dropped below 85% at Level 3. As a result, Jem would start on the *Bond Assessment Papers in Maths 9-10 years*, as there is work at Level 3 that Jem needs to understand before he can continue onto the *Bond Assessment Papers in Maths 10-11+* and *11+-12+*.

Once Jem has completed the *Bond Assessment Papers 11⁺-12⁺* in English and Maths, he can then concentrate on sitting the *11+ Test Papers*. As he will be sitting the 11+ standard format exam, he will work on the *Bond Standard Format 11+ Test Papers*. Here is his individual learning plan to reflect this:

Time Period	English	Maths
November	Bond Papers 10-11⁺ English	Bond Papers 9-10 Maths
December	Bond Papers 10-11⁺ English	Bond Papers 9-10Maths
January	Bond Papers 10-11⁺ English	Bond Papers 9-10Maths
February	Bond Papers 10-11⁺ English	Bond Papers 10-11⁺ Maths
March	Bond Papers 11⁺-12⁺ English	Bond Papers 10-11⁺ Maths
April	Bond Papers 11⁺-12⁺ English	Bond Papers 10-11⁺ Maths
May	Bond Papers 11⁺-12⁺ English	Bond Papers 10-11⁺ Maths
June	Bond Papers 11⁺-12⁺ English	Bond Papers 11⁺-12⁺ Maths
July	Bond Papers 11⁺-12⁺ English	Bond Papers 11⁺-12⁺ Maths
August	Bond Papers 11⁺-12⁺ English	Bond Papers 11⁺-12⁺ Maths
September	Bond 11+ Test Papers	Bond 11+ Test Papers
October	Bond 11+ Test Papers	Bond 11+ Test Papers

 What if Jem finishes a book before his timetable states?

The plan above isn't a set of rules, but a guide that offers some structure to a learning plan. If Jem finishes a book earlier, he can move onto the next book earlier or he can follow the motivational plan (see 'Motivate Your Child' page 73) to add fun to his learning package.

 What if Jem takes longer on a book than the plan suggests?

This would depend on how far behind Jem is with his plan. If he is taking longer because the work is too advanced, he may need to drop down a level first to ensure foundation work is thoroughly known. He may be falling behind because he is simply not completing enough work each week. If this is the case, the motivational plan is worth considering. It may simply be a minor hitch caused by home life or illness. The birth of another child, a family change, a house move or a broken leg can all disturb a routine that will soon settle down and usually, will have no long term effect on a learning plan as long as missed work is completed at a later stage. Sometimes a child feels overloaded with school homework, activities and family life, so 'extra' homework is left behind. In this instance a weekly timetable of priorities is often helpful, as well as making sure a child is not struggling with inappropriate work levels.

 Can Jem automatically move on when he has completed a paper?

Before a child attempts the next paper they need to fully understand why they have made mistakes and how to put the mistakes right. Going back over the paper and correcting it is a good indication of whether they really have understood the mistakes they have made. Copying the questions onto paper and asking your child to complete them the following day is also a good way of ensuring understanding is there, before your child continues with the next paper. If the problems are down to misreading the questions, take a look at the study ideas that can help your child to answer questions effectively.

 When Jem has completed a book, can he automatically move on to the next book?

No! The Bond series has a progress chart at the back of every book. When work is marked, the score can be entered into the progress chart. If a child is regularly scoring 85% and above, they are working at their optimum level and any mistakes can be looked at and revised before continuing with the next paper. If a child starts to fall below the 85% score line it suggests there are learning problems. This is what you are looking for, as this is the area that your child needs help with. Have they got a low score because they have misread a question/section or because they have a fundamental problem with understanding the material?

Develop Your Child's Learning Plan

To create your child's learning plan you need to find out the 11+ elements in your area and then look at the results for these subjects. Where does your child begin to struggle? By this, we mean when does your child drop below 85% on the Placement Tests? If your child scores above 85% on every area, then they are able to begin the *Bond Assessment Papers 11+-12+*. Otherwise, you will know what level books your child needs to start with for each subject area. You can then divide the number of books (one book per level for each subject needed) between the number of months you have left before the 11+ exam. Bear in mind that your child will need some time for practice test papers. As you monitor your child's progress, you can update the learning plan if necessary.

Here is a practice plan chart for you to make a personal learning plan. It covers a 12-month period, but depending on the time you have left, you could divide the time into months or weeks and spread the books and levels between this time.

Time Period	ENGLISH	MATHS	VR	NON-VR

If you have longer than 12 months, you might want to divide it into 6-week chunks, or however long you have. You may not need to study all four subject areas, so check which ones you need for your schools as they vary greatly from area to area. Be realistic about the amount of time you have left and the amount of work that needs to be completed.

Your ideal situation is to be studying two papers a week. This should allow for:

1   consolidation of work
2   new material with sufficient practise time
3   extended activities to supplement learning
4   practice papers to prepare for the 11+ exam.

Apply Bond's Step-by-Step Action Plans

Hannah's 11+ experience

We had no idea what the 11+ was like other than knowing that Wirral used the Verbal Reasoning Multiple-Choice Papers as their exam, but Michellejoy assessed Hannah and to our delight, Hannah gained high marks for the assessment. Michellejoy recommended Hannah start the Bond 10–11+ Years Papers in Verbal Reasoning, to build up her speed, and the 10–11+ Years Papers in Maths as this was Hannah's weakest area. We had six months until the 11+ exam and Hannah completed both books in eight weeks. We then put her onto the 10–11+ Years Papers in Verbal Reasoning, which took Hannah five weeks to complete. Michellejoy used the Bond Verbal Reasoning Multiple-Choice Test Papers and Hannah worked on these, getting better with each attempt. Her speed and confidence grew and on the day of her exam she was relaxed and knew what to expect.

The period of time between the exam and the results was difficult but Hannah busied herself with preparing for her SATs in school. We were thrilled when the 11+ results came through and Hannah passed. She went on to do really well with her SATs and is now happily settled into the school we hoped she would get in to. We will never know if Hannah would have passed the 11+ without following the Bond system, but we do know that she had the confidence and experience to sit the 11+ and that was definitely down to the Bond series. Now her little sister is in Year 4 we will be doing exactly the same with her.

John's 11+ experience

We felt John could do better at school as he was losing motivation, preferring football and friends to homework. We took him along to be assessed when he was in Year 4 and although John did well enough, Michellejoy was able to pinpoint problems in his English and maths. She recommended John begin the 9-10 Papers in Maths and English, which John followed. When he had completed these he moved onto the 10-11+ Papers in Maths and English and at that point we could really notice a difference in his school homework. John gained confidence and in Year 5 the school moved him up into the top set, which was a real motivating factor for him. He whizzed through the 11+-12+ Papers in Maths and English and also began the 10-11+ Papers in Verbal Reasoning.

When he came to sit the 11+ exam in the autumn term of Year 6, he was a motivated, confident boy who was enthusiastic and keen to pass.

We were thrilled when the results came through and John got into the school we wanted. He is now in his senior school and loving every minute of it. We managed to get the extra help John needed just at the right time. He was bright, but not outstanding and we know that the Bond series helped him to reach his full potential and to give him the start in life we wanted him to have. At the end of the day, one of the best gifts you can give your child is a good education.

Typical 12-month, 6-month and 3-month step-by-step action plans have been included here to help you, with advice if you have less or more time available. Find the plan that is closest to the period of time you have and use this as a template for your child's learning schedule.

(The following sections provide more details on elements such as recommended materials and the Bond Motivational Planner which are referred to in the action plans below).

12-month study plan for each subject to be covered

Months 1–3

First Quarter

1 Work through the Bond level books at learning plan pace.
2 Use the Bond *How to do* series for unknown areas of learning.
3 Use extended workbooks such as the Bond *No Nonsense* series to supplement learning.
4 Begin the motivational planner (see page 73).
5 Make notes of problematic areas that need further revision.

Months 4–6

Second Quarter

1 Continue with the Bond level books and the *How to do* series.
2 Strengthen problem areas with spelling lists, reading, logic puzzles, etc.
3 Use extended workbooks to supplement learning.
4 Revise learning plan if needed.
5 Continue the motivational planner.
6 Retest for spelling age to check progress.

Months 7–9

Third Quarter

1 Continue with the Bond final level books.

2 Use the *Bond How to do* series to strengthen weakest areas.

3 Introduce strict exam timings.

4 Continue the motivational planner.

5 Revise work in 'bite-size' chunks for daily revision. (The *Bond 10- Minute Tests* range can help to achieve this).

Months 10–12

Last Quarter

1 Use the *Bond 11+ Test Papers* to get used to exam format.

2 Tighten exam timings to allow time for checking.

3 Use the exam motivation programme.

4 Practise exam stress busters.

5 Strengthen any weak areas with 'bite-sized' chunks for daily revision. (Try the *Bond 10-Minute Tests* here.)

6 Final spelling age test to confirm progress made.

6-month study plan for each subject to be covered

Months 1–2

First Third

1 Work through the Bond level books at learning plan pace.

2 Use the *Bond How to do* series for unknown areas of learning.

3 Begin the motivational planner.

4 Make notes of problematic areas that need further revision.

Months 3–4

Second Third

1 Continue with the Bond level books.

2 Use the *Bond How to do* series to strengthen weakest areas and revise these on a daily basis.

3 Introduce strict exam timings.

4 Continue the motivational planner.

Months 5–6

Last Third

1 Continue with the Bond level papers highlighting any problem areas and concentrate on getting these areas right.

2 Use the *Bond 11+ Test Papers* to get used to exam format.

3 Keep to tight exam timings.

4 Use the exam motivation programme.

5 Practise exam stress busters.

6 Strengthen any weak areas using *Bond 10-Minute Tests*.

7 Retest for spelling age to check progress made so far.

3-month study plan for each subject to be covered

Month 1

First Month

1 Work through the relevant Bond level book.

2 Use the *Bond How to do* series for unknown areas of learning.

3 Begin the motivational planner.

4 Make notes of problematic areas that need further revision.

Month 2

Second Month

1 Work through the Bond final level book.

2 Work at keeping strict timings for each paper.

3 Use extended workbooks to supplement learning in problematic areas.

4 Continue the motivational planner.

Month 3

Third Month

1 Use *Bond 11+ Test Papers* to get used to exam format.

2 Keep to tight exam timings.

3 Use the exam motivation programme.

4 Practise exam stress busters.

5 Retest for spelling age to check progress made.

Suggestions for other time scales

More than 12 months to go

It is never too early to begin thinking about preparing for the 11+. The Bond range begins with Starter books for ages 6–7 and goes through to the 10–11+ age books. The series ensures children have a strong basis in maths, English, verbal and non-verbal reasoning. Here are some other key ways of developing 11+ skills from an early age:

- Establish a regular reading routine.
- Play and encourage educational games that extend your child's knowledge of words and definitions.
- Help your child to deal with numbers and shapes.
- Introduce games that develop logical thinking.

It is important in these early stages to keep learning fun and interesting so that your child doesn't become demotivated. With younger children refer to the Bond Starter books as quiz books and children will readily rise to the challenge of working through them, using the motivational chart as a score chart. It is best not to refer to the 11+ exam too early on, but to encourage a rounded educational experience for your child. It is a shame to see the learning experience as something only for schools to deal with, as children are open to all situations and will be influenced by everything that goes on around them.

Less than 3 months to go

If you have less than 3 months before the 11+ exam, it is important to focus on exam preparation. Look at the final stages of the suggested plans, which refer to exam timings, dealing with stress and working through test papers. If time allows, work through the *10–11+ Years Assessment Papers* for each subject to be studied, as this will give some practise at the types of question your child will need to answer.

At this stage, every single day counts, so even if you have only a week to go, work through at least two practice papers a day and one test paper. A crash course is not ideal but it is infinitely better than nothing, so make the most of the time available to ensure your child is as comfortable as possible with the format of the paper and the style of questions.

Recommended material

Bond Assessment Papers

These are the core Bond 11+ series books. There are five levels in total for each of the four 11+ subjects. The Bond Placement Tests will determine what level your child will begin working at in each subject. Each book consists of timed papers that provide extensive practice and constant revision of key areas. Each paper is carefully graded and there is a graph at the back of every book to chart progress. The series aims to consolidate, revise and prepare for the 11+ exams and for over 40 years, Bond has been the number one series for building towards the 11+.

Bond 'How to do' series

These books offer specific guidance on how to answer the full range of 11+ question types. There is one book for each subject and children can follow the step-by-step guides on how to approach each topic or question type. Examples of each element are provided and short practice activities can be completed to confirm understanding.

Bond 11+ Test Papers

These test papers cover all four subjects in both standard format and multiple-choice and provide an excellent means of gaining test experience. The easy-to-understand marking scheme offers the best way of gauging how your child has performed, and as each pack gives four individual tests, there is the ability to check progress.

Bond 10-Minute Tests

The *10 Minute Tests* provide bite-sized tests for quick practice and revision of all the key topics and question types for each of the four 11+ subjects. Tests focus on individual tricky question types, as well as covering a range of questions in the mixed tests. Each title also includes motivational devices such as puzzle pages and a scoring grid.

Bond 'No Nonsense' Maths and English

These books have been designed in line with the National Curriculum and offer a structured, rigorous step-by-step learning programme for 5–11 year olds. They give essential support for general practice as well as for 11+ preparation in these subjects. Maths and English underpin verbal and non-verbal reasoning, so these books can also be used to provide firm foundations for the skills and knowledge needed for these 11+ elements.

Extended workbooks

There are numerous books that can help with specific subjects. For example, the *Bond Personal Tutor* course and test papers are written specifically for the Verbal Reasoning element of the 11+ exam.

Schonell's Essential Spelling List and its three companion workbooks offer a structured spelling programme with exercises and puzzles to revise word lists.

(See Appendix B for full details of all of the above materials).

Extended activities

Anything that makes learning effective and fun is a useful aid in preparing children for the 11+. If you have the benefit of 12 months or more to prepare, your child can:

- complete jigsaw puzzles to help pattern formation and observation
- try word puzzles and crosswords to help with word patterns and spellings
- work through Suduko maths puzzles to help with logic and number work
- play board games such as Yahtzee and Scrabble to help develop transferable skills such as number work, word knowledge and logical thinking.

BEAM Education provide a wide range of educational games from tiny tots to teenagers (try http://www.beam.co.uk as a starting place). There are also a great many educational based CD roms and online games for children (try http://www.bbc.co.uk/schools/games/).

Motivate Your Child

The Bond Motivational Planner

> ❮ *I love doing the 11+ because I get weeks off with no homework and I get to earn prizes. My grandma was so pleased with my progress charts, she let me and my cousin have a sleep over. I took loads of hair bobbles and hair clips that I'd won and we had a really good time.* ❯
>
> (Sophie aged 10)

> ❮ *I love the Bond Motivational Planner because I never have to nag Sophie to do her work. Every week she works hard at her papers and she knows there are short and medium term rewards for her hard work, and long term, she knows she will be in the best possible position when she comes to take her 11+ test. I remember the misery of having to fit in extra homework when I took my 11+, but for Sophie, it's like a game. She can't see the rest of her future with adult eyes, but I will never again underestimate the power of a sparkly hair clip!* ❯
>
> (Sophie's Mum)

HINT

Some parents may feel wary of 'bribing' their children but it is far easier and more pleasant to reward than punish and aren't we preparing children for the adult world? For those of us with even the most rewarding of jobs, it might change the element of pleasure if we received no wages or remuneration for working overtime. Children of this age need to understand that the rewards are for doing extra work than what is expected of them normally. They also need to understand that it is for small, hard earned tokens not a computer game and pair of trainers every time they open a book.

The following planner works well with all children. It works on a credit/debit concept so that children can build up credits by doing extra work and then spend this credit on time off or cash it in for 'prizes'. It is very successful in promoting self-motivation and deals with the difficulty in keeping children focused.

There are two blank grids included in Appendix A, which you are free to photocopy for your own personal use, or to use as a template to create your own grid.

This is how the Bond motivational planner works:

1 Each week your child will be set their target (depending upon the time and work that needs to be covered this could be anything from one to seven papers). Each time your child completes this weekly target, they can colour in one square of the grid.

2 If they do one extra paper, they can colour in two squares as their target has a score of one square plus one 'bonus' square.

3 If a child completes two extra papers, they can colour in three squares as their target has a score of one square plus two 'bonus' squares, etc.

4 As a motivating factor for taking care and producing their best, children can be rewarded with an extra bonus square every time they reach 100% in a paper.

5 When they complete a book, they are awarded five extra bonus squares.

This system means a child can choose to colour in the grid quicker than planned and can therefore 'cash in' their grid sooner. Once a month it becomes 'dice week' (although rolling one die is infinitely cheaper than two dice!):

1 Your child rolls the dice.

2 Whatever the number is, that becomes the multiplier of papers completed that week.

3 For example, if the dice rolls a six and your child does three papers, they get 18 squares coloured in. If the dice rolls a four and your child does two papers, they get eight squares to colour in.

Here is an example of Nishpa's paper for this month:

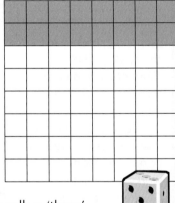

Week 1: Nishpa's target was one English and one Verbal Reasoning paper. She completed this target and coloured in one square. She also achieved 100% in her Verbal Reasoning Paper and received an extra bonus square for this.

Week 2: Nishpa had the same target but she only completed one paper. Because she did not reach her target she couldn't colour in a square.

Week 3: Nishpa's target was two English and one Verbal Reasoning paper. She completed two English and two Verbal Reasoning and so she coloured in one square for completing her target and one square for doing an extra paper.

Week 4: This week it is 'dice week'. Nishpa rolls a 'three'. Her target was one English and one Verbal Reasoning paper. She did two English and three Verbal Reasoning papers so she coloured in three squares for completing her target (1 × dice roll of 3) plus nine squares for exceeding her target (3 × dice roll of 3) giving her a weekly total of 12.

You would be amazed how motivating this grid system is. When a child reaches 50 squares they can 'take off' any two days. When a child reaches 100 squares they can take a week off and receive a suitable prize (for example a £5 book token/cinema voucher or a small present such as gel pens, trading cards, Beanie Baby, hair bobbles, book, torch, poster, etc.). You will know the type of gift your child would appreciate most.

Q *Why use a motivational system like this?*

If you are made to work on something every week with no break for month after month you would soon get fed up and resentful. If you were made to work on something every day and were offered a break and a reward, you would work with a spring in your step and a smile. Children are no different, and even when they know it is good for them to spend time on their education, they have school during the day, homework afterwards and then we ask them to do even more homework during the week. It is far better to sacrifice the odd small gift that has been justly earned and to allow them a week of no work.

Q *I'm desperate for my child to do well and would feel irritated to see them wasting time on a week off.*

If your child does the bare minimum each week, they will take a long time to reach the 100 squares. If they choose to complete extra work to get there quicker, they are still completing the same amount of work and they need to be rewarded for this. If not, there is no incentive for doing extra. It is important, as a parent, to keep telling a child how well they have done to 'earn' this privilege and to reinforce that it is down to their hard work that they have enough 'credit' to now spend it. You are teaching your child so many transferable skills this way, such as the ability to put in effort now to gain something worthwhile later. You are teaching them to feel proud of their achievements, to emphasise that they are hard working and conscientious and that they can achieve the goals that have been set.

Q *What if my child is still reluctant to complete work?*

Confirming the need to work steadily in order to achieve 11+ knowledge and confidence is important. If your child feels in control of their learning scheme they are far more likely to agree to the regular homework that is needed. Involving them at the planning stage is therefore vital if they are to see what needs to be achieved and in what time frame. Reminding your child throughout this preparation process, that they are working well and will soon be able to have some time off, or a prize for their endeavour will keep them focused. Having the grid filled in each week and using the 'dice week' allows them to see how far and how fast they are progressing.

Q *I know my child will rush through the papers without consideration in order to achieve the reward. How do I get them to do their best?*

Remind your child that if they achieve below 85% they will have to redo the paper (but still award their bonus mark), but if it is clear that they have rushed the paper and not taken care, they will forfeit the right to their bonus square. Always err on the side of caution here and only do this if you are certain that your child has rushed through the paper.

Q *Can I take squares off when my child misbehaves at home or school?*

If a child feels that every misdemeanour will result in reduced squares, the system becomes less motivational and more punishment based. In the same way, if good behaviour is to be rewarded, this is not the place to do it, otherwise the purpose of rewarding extra 11+

work is lost. I think it is really important that this motivational planner is kept purely for 11+ preparation work.

 My child makes constant 'silly' mistakes like missing out an odd question or not filling in the paper correctly.

An effective way of dealing with this problem is to encourage your child to go through their paper each time they finish one and to mark off each question as they check it using a different coloured pen. When they can see how many 'silly' mistakes they have made, it helps reduce the problem significantly, and again, reward with a bonus square when they have checked their paper.

 My child is very downhearted when their progress dips below 85%. How can I keep them motivated when this happens?

The Bond books have a progress chart in the back, which is filled in each time a paper is marked. Being able to see a long-term view of progress made, a child can see that the odd paper that achieves less than is desired is not a major problem. By reminding your child of their long-term progress you are making it clear that:

1   you are not disappointed in them and their poorer score
2   the score is a positive way of highlighting problem areas
3   these problem areas are now resolved which shows effective learning
4   some papers score poorer than others which is how it should be
5   the overall score is the important one, not the individual paper scores.

 My child is getting lower and lower scores. What do I do?

Your child may be struggling with some of the concepts for particular question types and these areas need to be resolved. Try working through the *How to do* books and see if that helps. Also make sure that they are not working on books that are too advanced for them.

It is worth checking back to the Placement Tests Results Chart, to ensure your child is working at the appropriate level for each subject according to these results. If your child has not yet sat the Bond Placement Tests, this is the time they need to do so in order to clarify their ability levels. It is also important to check that when a child has achieved less than 85% on a paper, that they have gone back through it and corrected any problems, making sure they understand the type of question they are getting wrong.

Minimise Stress for Everyone

When a child is preparing for the 11+ exam, the whole family are affected. There are ways to minimise potential problems by planning ahead and using the TEAM system.

Time – **Expectations** – **Atmosphere** – **Management**

Time

1 Allow sufficient time for your child to prepare for the 11+.

2 Organise the learning plan for progress without pressure.

3 Find a working timetable that gives your child time to sit papers each week without them feeling overloaded.

4 Help your child to make study a regular routine.

Expectations

1 Be realistic about your child's 11+ potential.

2 Be open with your child in communication so that you each know how the other is feeling and what your concerns are.

3 Avoid comparing your child to other children/siblings.

4 Avoid constantly talking about secondary schools.

Atmosphere

1 Let your child know that you value them and are proud of them regardless of how they perform in the 11+ exam.

2 When your child is upset or argumentative, check if this is down to a lack of understanding in their 11+ work.

3 Take the 11+ seriously by marking your child's work, taking time to give feedback and by listening to the concerns they might have.

4 Offer encouragement in conjunction with the motivational planner.

5 Try not to talk repeatedly about the 11+ when your child is relaxing, taking a break or when they have 'earned' some time off study.

Management

1 Find a quiet space for your child to work.

2 Check they have everything they need for their study time.

3 Ensure your child has the correct books as and when they are needed and ensure they aren't weighed down with every 11+ book, CD and online site offered by 'helpful' people.

> **? HINT**
>
> *It can sometimes be difficult to tell whether your child is suffering from stress, but some of the main symptoms include: tearfulness, aches and pains, headaches, irritable bowels or bladder, moodiness, introversion, change of appetite, disturbed sleep and an aggravation of present ailments such as asthma, allergies or eczema.*
>
> *If you or other family members also suffer with any of these effects of stress please do take it seriously. Take time out to do something relaxing and eat, drink and sleep properly. Take regular slots of activity and above all, keep communication open. Talking to friends or extended family about how you feel can relieve the symptoms of stress.*

Deal With the Exam Day

There are huge differences between primary schools and how they treat the 11+ exam. In some schools pupils are actively coached and given plenty of test papers, while in other schools, your child might be the only one taking the 11+ and the school will make no reference to it. Ideally your child will have at least one mock paper under exam conditions and will know what to expect, but if not make sure your child has the following information:

1 Your child knows the format of the exam, the subjects to be tested and the date/time/place of the exam.

2 Remind your child that they have done practice papers and are used to the format of the exam they are taking.

3 Confirm that your child knows how to fill in their name and age on the answer paper although this will be mentioned when they are in the exam room itself.

4 Give your child the opportunity to get a good night's sleep.

5 Ensure your child gets up in time, has a nutritious breakfast and is feeling as confident as possible.

6 Check your child has pencil/eraser/ruler/pencil sharpener/tissues and glasses if they need them or any inhalers or medication.

7 Encourage them to use the toilet before entering the exam room and make sure they know where the toilet is before they start the test.

8 Remind them to find the clock before they start so that they can make time checks during the exam.

9 Arrive at the exam in plenty of time.

10 Wish them well but remind them that they have prepared sufficiently for this exam, they have worked to the best of their ability and that you are confident that they will now perform the best that they can.

TRY THIS!

It is worth checking the *Bond How to do* series in Maths and English as they have details on dealing with the run up to the exam and about the exam day itself.

 Help! My child has woken up with a raging temperature/chicken pox/has just broken their leg, etc.

Don't panic! It is usual practise that if a child is too ill to take the 11+ exam, they will be given an opportunity at a later date to sit the test. This isn't an ideal situation but it is one that is easily dealt with, so please don't worry.

Checklist for Step 3 Success

☐ I've created a learning plan for my child

☐ I know how to motivate my child

☐ I know how to recognise and manage stress effectively

☐ I know how to cope with the exam day itself

I still need to find out more about ....

....

....

....

....

....

STEP 4
Manage the Post-Exam Process

❝ I hadn't realised how stressful the post-exam period was. We had been so geared up in preparing for the 11+ that there was a real anti-climax afterwards and all we could do was sit, wait and imagine, and the imagining was the worst...❞

❝ I was so glad we had an effective study timetable in place. We continued this with SATs preparation to keep us busy and as a distraction from thinking about the results. This study method really helped my daughter to settle into the homework routine at secondary school, so I'm glad we kept going during those crucial 'after 11+' months. ❞

4

Plan for What Happens Next

The results are out about 10–16 weeks after the exam and this time is like living in limbo. There is nothing you can do, nothing you can plan for and you feel helpless, right? Wrong! There is much that you can do:

• Understand how the appeals process works.

• Ensure that your child is ready to cope with secondary school.

• Decode the results.

• Know what to do if your child fails.

• Deal with the 'in limbo' stress.

Let's deal with the most immediate feelings. You may feel relief that the exam is over and so give your child and yourself time to recover and relax a little. A day out or an activity you can work on together is a nice way of reaffirming the bond you have with your child and can make them feel much less nervous about the waiting period.

Decode the Results and Appeals Process

One of the most common questions asked is 'What is the pass mark?' and this is soon followed by 'What can I do if my child fails the 11+?' Knowing in advance how the exams are marked and what you can do will help alleviate the worry. When you receive your child's results and offer of a school, you will also receive details on the appeals procedure and the strict timetable that you will need to follow in order to accept an offer or to begin an appeal. Some of the most common questions about results and appeals are outlined below.

Frequently Asked Questions About the Results

 When do the results come through and what do they say?
The result time varies from authority to authority but the results are usually through within 16 weeks. You will be given a date when the results are due and, depending upon which school you have put first on your LEA list, you will be offered a place at that school if your child has passed. If they have not got into their first school of choice, you may well be offered the second, third or other choice.

Q *What is the pass mark?*

The number of school places that are available sets the pass mark. If a school has 200 places then the top 200 test marks get in. This does mean that the pass mark can vary from year to year. There will also be variations in the birth rate for individual years, so if there are a lot of boys in your son's year and you have applied for a boys' school, there will be more boys fighting for available places, whilst girls in the same academic year might have far fewer pupils going for the available places.

Q *My child is 11 months younger than her friend so how can the marking be fair?*

In most 11+ areas, exam papers are marked and scores are standardised by age, this means that there are allowances made for the age of the child so that each child can be fairly assessed.

Q *What does standardisation mean?*

All of the exam papers have a 'raw score', which is quite literally something like 78/85 or 69/80 and means the total number of correct answers compared to the maximum score available. Then the child's age is added to the equation and the raw score turned into a grade. A child who has a score of 75/80 and is 10 years and 3 months might get a final score of 130, whilst a child who also has 75/80 but who is 10 years and 6 months, might get a final score of 125. Obviously there is no definitive answer here as every exam board has their own way of marking that may, or may not, include standardisation.

Q *What is the computer marking system and how reliable is it?*

Multiple-choice answer papers can be fed into a computer and marked as the computer 'looks' for the boxes with pencil marks in to award marks. This is a fast system and is very reliable, as computers don't yet suffer with human error. It does mean however, that your child must mark the boxes on the multiple-choice answer sheet carefully.

Q *What if my child gets just under the pass mark?*

There is often a schools' waiting list for the next highest scoring children. Some pupils may have sat the entrance exam for a number of schools and so may opt out of the one you have chosen. If this happens, the top score on the waiting list gets in.

Q *How does the over subscription criteria work?*

If a school is over subscribed, a criterion is put in place to select pupils. You will find information on this in your school prospectus, but the usual reasons that a school will give can include any or all of the following in any order the school presets:

1 How far you live from the school.
2 Siblings who may already be in the school.
3 Places for children in care.
4 Places for children with special or educational needs.
5 Children of a certain religious faith.

6 Children who achieved a certain grade in music.
7 Children who have excelled in sport.
8 Children who have other family connections to the school.

Frequently Asked Questions About the Appeal

 Is there anything else I can do to get my child into the school of my choice?

Some schools have several routes into a school; an academic entrance exam or a music or sport place for example. If your child fails the academic route is there another route that your child might be eligible for? If not, other children above your child on the waiting list might take up vacant places so that your child moves up a position. Even when the school year starts some pupils will move house or suddenly start another school instead, so if you are really keen to get your child into the school there is an outside chance that a place may be available. However, this can be a stressful situation to be in and you may prefer to end the tension and go for the school offered by your LEA.

 My child didn't perform well. Can we appeal?

This depends on the reason why your child didn't do well. All schools have a policy on their appeals process, and if this is a route you wish to take, you need to contact the school as soon as possible and ask for advice on their appeals system (although when you receive your school offer, you should receive information about appealing and the time frame given). You will probably be advised to wait until the test results are through, but it is wise to inform the test centre as soon as possible after the exam if the reason is illness. If a school is aware that a child took the exam and was then sent to the doctor that day because they developed mumps, it is better than a retrospective appeal three months later.

 How can I look at my child's marked 11+ paper to ensure it has been fairly marked?

With most examinations (SATs, 11+, GCSE, 'A' level etc) it is not possible for you to see a marked script. There are many reasons for this, including administrative limitations and the psychological effect for a child knowing there may be 'come back' from the parent, however well meaning. The Freedom of Information Act (FoIA) has to be followed by all schools and authorities and they will have strict guidelines on what can and can't be revealed. What you can do is request your child's paper to be remarked by hand, but it is virtually unheard of for any child to have their score changed because of this, probably because of the accuracy of the computerised marking system.

> ◄ We waited nervously from December until the results were through on 1 March and we were so pleased that Marie-Anne was offered our first choice of the grammar school. The previous year our eldest daughter Rachael wasn't offered a place because she was short of 3 marks. We had to wait for another six weeks and we had begun to wish we had taken the school offered by the LEA as we were nervous about appealing in case it had a negative effect on Rachael. Then we were offered a place at the grammar school, as we were high on the waiting list. We are so glad we appealed and now both girls are together at the grammar school doing well... ►

> ◄ We decided to lodge an appeal because we didn't want Raj to go to any other school and, because he failed to get a high enough mark, we had no other viable option. The whole situation dragged on for weeks and in the end, we were turned down. We tried then to appeal for our second choice of school but that was also oversubscribed and our appeal failed. We really wished we had put more schools down as we were then stuck with the school the LEA wanted us to go to. We still weren't happy and Raj had no school to go to in the September. Eventually he went to another school that we were happy enough with, but not until the November, and by then he had missed lots of schooling and our childcare arrangements for looking after Raj drove us close to the edge. We found out that you can only appeal against schools you have down on your original list, so when his little brother is ready, we will put down the maximum number of schools and unless he is close to the pass mark, we won't go through an appeal again... ►

So is it worth appealing or not? It is such a difficult decision to make, but I would suggest you look long and hard at the prospectus first. Look at the over subscription criterion and see how likely you are to be selected on these grounds. Also look at the grade your child has, and if they are very close to the pass mark, it may well be worth appealing. If your child has a low mark and you don't fit into any of the criteria for over subscription, your chance of appealing is far more limited. It's a difficult balance between realism and hope and there will be many parents who decide the added stress is not worth it. The more parents who make this decision, the more pupils will be removed from the list of potential appealers so bear this in mind if you are appealing.

Prepare for Secondary School

Whatever school your child attends, you want them to be as prepared as possible and that means getting through SATs with as good a grade as possible. In some secondary schools, they will place pupils immediately into academic sets based on the SATs results so it is worth continuing with maths and English to ensure this is as good as possible. Science is the other SATs subject so strengthening these three areas is a good focus while you are waiting for exam results. Your child has probably got a good studying routine in place, so this can be utilised with any of the SATs preparation books or the *Bond Get Ready For Secondary School* series in maths and English.

So what activities can help your child prepare for Secondary School? Here are some examples that have worked well for many pupils.

The English SATS exam has a short and long writing test and both require extended reading skills. Now might be a good time to get a reading plan in place. This could include a trip to the library or a bookshop and making a reading list that your child would like to work through. Including your child in this choosing process, and in setting a suitable time for their reading, means they are far more likely to take part than in an enforced scheme of work.

Letter writing is a popular form of extended writing used in the SATS. Encouraging your child to write letters to friends and pen friends or to thank people for presents is a useful way of introducing these skills in a real environment. A most effective form of learning is when your child isn't aware that that is what they are doing!

Playing board games such as Scrabble, Monopoly, Cluedo, etc. can help a child to develop transferable skills of calculation, word knowledge or logical thinking.

Activities To Prepare For Secondary School

Although children will have trips out with school, insurance concerns mean that children are more limited to where and when they go. At this age most museums, especially the "hands on" ones, are perfect for children and the interactive elements make learning fun.

Instead of using the computer as a games machine, encourage your child to research topics on the Internet. The BBC website is geared up for SATs with educational games and web pages linked to their favourite hobbies or television programmes.

Make the most of any learning experience through practical situations. Decorating a room requires measurement, size and cost calculations as does preparing sufficient food for a party of a set number of people at a given budget. Planning the family holiday (real or dreamed!) is another clever means of developing your child's skills.

There are some great websites available for interactive learning and English, maths and science games. For SATs preparation, the following are well worth a visit:
www.beam.co.uk
www.brightminds.co.uk
www.bbc.co.uk
www.curriculumonline.gov.uk

Manage Stress

The same feelings of stress can occur during this post-exam period for your child and indeed the whole family. Reliving nightmares or feeling scared of planning for the future is difficult to deal with. Useful techniques include the following:

Support

1 Reassure your child that you love them regardless of how they perform.

1 Listen to their concerns and worries.

1 Encourage them to focus beyond the 11+ to more immediate distractions.

Focus

1 Help your child to enjoy all areas of their life.

1 Encourage them to throw themselves into their hobbies and interests.

1 Ensure your child has a balanced lifestyle with sufficient sleep, nourishment and activity.

Plan

1 Devise plans of what will happen in the event of your child passing the 11+, and if they don't.

1 Focus on the positives of both plans.

1 Get your child involved in this planning to make them feel less passive.

Prepare

1 Work towards good SATS grades.

1 Begin (or continue to develop) a reading list.

1 Encourage your child to retain a positive view of school by making the most of the primary school year they have left.

Final thoughts

Following the system prescribed in this manual will prepare you and your child as well as possible for the 11+ and beyond. The 11+ isn't about being a success or being a failure, it's about finding the right school and the right educational environment for your child. Your child might pass or fail the criteria for an individual school's entrance policy but that doesn't make reference to the rest of their life. There are plenty of bright children who do fantastically well having failed the 11+ exam and plenty of children who have passed the 11+ exam and are sadly not living a happy and successful life. Making your child aware that success comes from working to the best of their own potential and reaching their own standards and goals is perhaps the best message you can convey to them.

I hope you have found this book informative and useful and I wish you and your child every success for the future.

Michellejoy

APPENDIX A
Bond's Motivational Planner

<table>
<tr><td>Date:</td><td></td></tr>
</table>

								10
								20
								30
								40
								50
								60
								70
								80
								90
								100

Date:

								10
								20
								30
								40
								50
								60
								70
								80
								90
								100

Photocopy these grids for your own personal use or use them as a template for your own grid.

APPENDIX B
Essential Resources

Summaries of the essential resources that you can use to support your child's 11+ preparation are given below, while further details are noted in the tables that follow.

The Bond Series

The Bond 11+ range consists of *How to do* books, one in each of the 11+ subjects. There are practical workbooks which begin with the *Assessment Papers* for *6–7 years* and continue through books 1–5 in each of the four 11+ subjects. Bond completes the series with *11+ Test Papers* in each subject, both in standard format and multiple-choice, a range of *10 Minute Tests* which are ideal for bite-sized revision and two titles in maths and English which help to bridge the gap between primary and secondary school and boost your child's confidence. All of these books can be bought or ordered from bookshops or direct from the Nelson Thornes website (www.nelsonthornes.com).

BOND TITLES		ISBN
How to do . . . 11+ English		9780748796953
Assessment Papers in English 5–6 years		9780748784646
Assessment Papers in English 6–7 years		9780748784974
Assessment Papers in English 7–8 years		9780748781058
Assessment Papers in English 8–9 years		9780748781225
Assessment Papers in English 9–10 years Book 1		9780748781126
Assessment Papers in English 9–10 years Book 2		9780748784660
Assessment Papers in English 10–11+ years Book 1		9780748781164
Assessment Papers in English 10–11+ years Book 2		9780748784707
Assessment Papers in English 11+–12+ years Book 1		9780748784837
Assessment Papers in English 11+–12+ years Book 2		9780748784745
Assessment Papers in English 12+–13+ years		9780748784783
11+ Test Papers	(Standard)	9780748784882
11+ Test Papers	(Multiple-choice)	9780748784875
10 Minute Tests in English	(9–10 years)	9780748798964
10 Minute Tests in English	(10–11+ years)	9780748796977
10 Minute Tests in English	(11+–12+ years)	9780748799008
Get Ready for Secondary School: English		9780748775392

BOND TITLES		ISBN
How to do ... 11+ Maths		9780748796960
Assessment Papers in Maths 5–6 years		9780748784653
Assessment Papers in Maths 6–7 years		9780748784981
Assessment Papers in Maths 7–8 years		9780748781065
Assessment Papers in Maths 8–9 years		9780748781096
Assessment Papers in Maths 9–10 years Book 1		9780748781133
Assessment Papers in Maths 9–10 years Book 2		9780748784677
Assessment Papers in Maths 10–11+ years Book 1		9780748781171
Assessment Papers in Maths 10–11+ years Book 2		9780748784714
Assessment Papers in Maths 11+–12+ years Book 1		9780748784844
Assessment Papers in Maths 11+–12+ years Book 2		9780748784752
Assessment Papers in Maths 12+–13+ years		9780748784790
11+ Test Papers	(Standard)	9780748784899
11+ Test Papers	(Multiple-choice)	9780748784820
10 Minute Tests in Maths	(9–10 years)	9780748798971
10 Minute Tests in Maths	(10–11+ years)	9780748796984
10 Minute Tests in Maths	(11+–12+ years)	9780748799015
Get Ready for Secondary School: Maths		9780748775385

BOND TITLES		ISBN
How to do ... 11+ Verbal Reasoning		9780748784967
Assessment Papers in Verbal Reasoning 6–7 years		9780748784998
Assessment Papers in Verbal Reasoning 7–8 years		9780748781072
Assessment Papers in Verbal Reasoning 8–9 years		9780748781102
Assessment Papers in Verbal Reasoning 9–10 years Book 1		9780748781140
Assessment Papers in Verbal Reasoning 9–10 years Book 2		9780748784691
Assessment Papers in Verbal Reasoning 10–11+ years Book 1		9780748781188
Assessment Papers in Verbal Reasoning 10–11+ years Book 2		9780748784738
Assessment Papers in Verbal Reasoning 11+–12+ years Book 1		9780748784851
Assessment Papers in Verbal Reasoning 11+–12+ years Book 2		9780748784776
11+ Test Papers	(Standard)	9780748784936
11+ Test Papers	(Multiple-choice)	9780748784929
10 Minute Tests in Verbal Reasoning	(9–10 years)	9780748798988
10 Minute Tests in Verbal Reasoning	(10–11+ years)	9780748797009
10 Minute Tests in Verbal Reasoning	(11+–12+ years)	9780748799022

BOND TITLES	ISBN
How to do ... 11+ Non-verbal Reasoning Ω	9780748781218
Assessment Papers in Non-verbal Reasoning 6–7 years	9780748781041
Assessment Papers in Non-verbal Reasoning 7–8 years	9780748781089
Assessment Papers in Non-verbal Reasoning 8–9 years	9780748781119
Assessment Papers in Non-verbal Reasoning 9–10 years Book 1	9780748781157
Assessment Papers in Non-verbal Reasoning 9–10 years Book 2	9780748784684
Assessment Papers in Non-verbal Reasoning 10–11+ years Book 1	9780748781232
Assessment Papers in Non-verbal Reasoning 10–11+ years Book 2	9780748784721
Assessment Papers in Non-verbal Reasoning 11+–12+ years Book 1	9780748784868
Assessment Papers in Non-verbal Reasoning 11+–12+ years Book 2	9780748784769
11+ Test Papers (Standard)	9780748784943
11+ Test Papers (Multiple-choice)	9780748784950
10 Minute Tests in Non-verbal Reasoning (9–10 years)	9780748798995
10 Minute Tests in Non-verbal Reasoning (10–11+ years)	9780748796991
10 Minute Tests in Non-verbal Reasoning (11+–12+ years)	9780748799039

11+ Personal Tutor

The *11+ Personal Tutor* range offers a step-by-step programme that is split into seven full-colour lessons covering all the key skills needed for 11+ verbal reasoning exams. Packs of four standard and four multiple-choice papers support the course teaching, which offer additional practice in an exam format.

TITLES	ISBN
11+ Personal Tutor Verbal Reasoning Course	074876724X
11+ Personal Tutor Verbal Reasoning Papers (Standard)	0748767290
11+ Personal Tutor Verbal Reasoning Papers (Multiple-choice)	0748767304

Bond No Nonsense

Bond No Nonsense is a home learning series for 5–11 year-olds that provides clear and straightforward teaching and learning for maths and English in a rigorous, step-by-step manner. Each book offers a well-structured learning experience that avoids the use of distracting gimmicks such as cartoons.

BOND NO NONSENSE ENGLISH	ISBN
Ages 5–6	0748795626
Ages 6–7	0748795634
Ages 7–8	0748795642
Ages 8–9	0748795650
Ages 9–10	0748795669
Ages 10–11	0748795677

BOND NO NONSENSE MATHS	ISBN
Ages 5–6	0748795685
Ages 6–7	0748795693
Ages 7–8	0748795707
Ages 8–9	0748795715
Ages 9–10	0748795723
Ages 10–11	0748795731

Schonell's Essential Spelling series

This series offers the *Essential Spelling List*, which includes over 3000 words that children often need in their writing tasks, and three *Essential Spelling* workbooks, which provide additional practice of key words and phrases through a variety of different activities. The *Essential Spelling List* also includes guidance on how to work out a spelling age.

TITLES	ISBN
The Essential Spelling List	0174244932
The Essential Spelling Book 1	017424083X
The Essential Spelling Book 2	0174240821
The Essential Spelling Book 3	0174240813

APPENDIX C
Answers to Bond Placement Tests

Your child must have an answer 100% correct to receive a mark. There are no half marks for almost right answers.

Verbal Reasoning Level 1

1 D50; **2** 35D; **3** 11; **4** 32; **5** 6; **6** 2; **7** woman; **8** low; **9** mate, team; **10** seat, teas.

Verbal Reasoning Level 2

1 yawned, tired, bed; **2** lights, dark; **3** brief, short; **4** talk, speak; **5** help, less; **6** in, doors; **7** art; **8** low; **9** T; **10** H.

Verbal Reasoning Level 3

1 shorten;   **2** follow;   **3** forgive;   **4** ice;   **5** up;   **6** green;   **7** pot, turned;   **8** wilting, hot;   **9** wait, sit;   **10** green;   **11** serve;   **12** sheen;   **13** 3;   **14** 755;   **15** 125.

Verbal Reasoning Level 4

1 reward, punishment;   **2** free, enslave;   **3** perfect, flawed;   **4** precious, precise, present, prettier, pretty;   **5** graceful, gracious, graph, graphic, graphite;   **6** lard;   **7** very;   **8** soda;   **9** MPTF;   **10** IPMF;   **11** 28;   **12** 35;   **13** Tap;   **14** Julie;   **15** Julie, Jemima.

English Level 1

1 I;   **2** she;   **3** foul – to break the rules, daffodil – a spring flower, foal – a baby horse, reptile – a cold-blooded animal;   **4** several – more than a few but not all, nostril – opening at the end of your nose, server – someone who serves, smoke – cloud of gas and small bits of solid material;   **5** clear;   **6** patient;   **7** was;   **8** drank;   **9** helped;   **10** did.

English Level 2

1 drink;   **2** creep;   **3** Daniel's rabbit;   **4** The milkman's overalls;   **5** 1b; 2a, 3c;   **6** 1b, 2c, 3a;

Any two words chosen from these lists:

7 Noun: bull, Sompiti, grass, eyes, dress;   **8** Verb: looked, deciding, carried, chewing, took, stepped, wanting, wished, chosen, wear, made, hang;   **9** Adverb: slow, never, carefully, back, around;   **10** Adjective: brown, big, dark, long, red.

English Level 3

*Your child may word **1–5** differently as long as the key words are there. It is acceptable in **1** to answer 'White fluffy sheep' and for **2** to answer 'sun,' for example. In **5** any acceptable answer receives a mark and in **6–9** and **14–15** any words selected from those given is to be awarded a mark. There are no half marks for almost correct answers.*

1 'White fluffy sheep, scampering through the sky';   **2** Sunlight, sunshine or rays of the sun;   **3** Green frothy bubbles bend and squash under my feet;   **4** There are no leaves left and the branches are blowing in the breeze;   **5** Any answer that describes a part of the poem with a reason why;   **6** but, although;   **7** and, so, because;   **8** when, as, until, before, so;   **9** outside, outlet, outhouse, inlet, inside, without, within, ringlet, ringside, greenhouse;   **10** silvery, slippery;   **11** library, equipped;   **12** might, magazine;   **Q13** tried, separate;   **14** reminded, reminding, reminder;   **15** unequalled, inequality, inequalities.

English Level 4

*For **1–4** an answer that means the same as the given answer is acceptable. In **6–7** any words selected from those given is to be awarded a mark. There are no half marks for almost correct answers.*

1 To oil, to allow free movement, to moisten;   **2** To reduce, to shorten, to make smaller;   **3** To fix a problem or issue, to find a conclusion, to bring an image into focus or to make up one's mind to do something;   **4** castle;   **5** moat;   **6** tongue; **7** wondered;   **8** persuaded;   **9** Proper nouns: Macbeth, Wednesday; **10** Collective nouns: team, class;   **11** Pair of antonyms: can/cannot, never/always, best/worst;   **12** Pair of homophones: read/red, seen/scene, too/to;   **13** *Any six of the following (other words may also be acceptable):* recalled, muttered, whispered, thought, supposed, alleged, held, believed, understood, assumed, explained, articulated, reported, told, uttered, stuttered, responded, moaned, spat, hissed, shouted, yelled, retorted, mentioned, referred, mouthed, lilted, communicated, expressed;   **14** Tom had asked if he was ready yet. Tom asked him if he was ready; **15** There are many people who say, 'Why bother with exams?' They're aware of the importance of qualifications, but can't understand why one bad day could ruin the rest of your future. I would agree in part to this, but say, 'A well prepared pupil will always fare better than one who is relying on luck.'

Maths Level 1

1 24;   **2** 1007;   **3** > >;   **4** < >;   **5** 40 79;   **6** 19 63;   **7** 7;   **8** 49;   **9** 9; **10** 48.

Maths Level 2

1 370 m;   **2** 325 m;   **3** 3;   **4** 5 20;   **5** 20 30 40;   **6** 15 30 60;   **7 A** Octagon, **B** Pentagon, **C** Parallelogram;   **8** 5, 15, 45, 55, 120

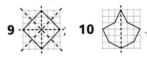

9 ;   **10** .

Maths Level 3

1 8.5 10;   **2** 42 22;   **3** 36 45;   **4** 3276;   **5** 1808;   **6** 2976;   **7** 8883;   **8** 10 000; **9** 0.1;   **10** 4.72;   **11** B A   **12** A C;   **13** 48 cm;   **14** 143 154;   **15** 20 30.

Maths Level 4

1 8.01;   **2** 540;   **3** $1\frac{1}{4}$;   **4: A** 12, **B** 12, **C** 8, **D** 24;   **5: A** 8, **B** 8, **C** 5, **D** 16; **6: A** 5, **B** 6, **C** 6, **D** 10;   **7: A** 54 cm^2, **B** 48 cm^2;   **8: A** 27 cm^3, **B** 20 cm^3;   **9**: £58.85, £11.31;   **10**: £6.10;   **11**: £4.75, £38.75; **12** $3\frac{1}{8}$ or $\frac{25}{8}$ or $3\frac{125}{1000}$ **13** $7\frac{5}{8}$ or $\frac{61}{8}$ or $7\frac{625}{1000}$;   **14** $4\frac{1}{20}$ or $\frac{81}{20}$ or $4\frac{5}{100}$; **15** $9\frac{15}{200}$ or $9\frac{75}{1000}$ or $\frac{363}{40}$ or $9\frac{3}{40}$.

Non-Verbal Reasoning Level 1

1 b; **2** a; **3** d; **4** a; **5** ; **6** ; **7** c; **8** b; **9** b; **10** d.

Non-Verbal Reasoning Level 2

1 b; **2** d; **3** d; **4** a; **5** a; **6** d; **7** e; **8** c; **9** b; **10** a, e.

Non-Verbal Reasoning Level 3

1 c; **2** a; **3** e; **4** b; **5** a; **6** b; **7** a; **8** a; **9** e; **10** c; **11** d; **12** c; **13** CZ; **14** R2; **15** D1.

Non-Verbal Reasoning Level 4

1 e; **2** c; **3** Z14; **4** M5; **5** GG; **6** e; **7** e; **8** f; **9** e; **10** e; **11** d; **12** d; **13** d; **14** a; **15** b.

Please visit www.bond11plus.co.uk and follow the Free Resources link to access the following useful information:

1 Contact details of UK **Grammar schools** (including telephone no. and email address) and the 11+ subjects each school sets.

2 Contact details (location and telephone no.) of UK **Independent schools**.

3 Contact details (telephone no. and website address) of UK **LEAs**.